DECIDE

How to Manage the Risk in Your Decision Making

DECIDE

How to Manage the Risk in Your Decision Making

BRYAN WHITEFIELD

Published by Bryan Whitefield Consulting
PO Box 7367 Warringah Mall
Brookvale NSW 2100 Australia
www.bryanwhitefield.com
Copyright © 2015 Bryan Whitefield
Bryan Whitefield asserts the moral right to be identified as the author of this work.
First Published November 2015

ISBN 978-0-646-94767-9

Cover design and illustrations by David Williams. davidw57@optusnet.com.au
Edited by Caroline Falls, Alexander Falls Productions, Sydney, Australia. caroline@
afpcontent.com
Typesetting by Peter Guo, letterspaced typesetting. www.letterspaced.com.au
Printed by IngramSpark. www.ingramspark.com

Table of Contents

List of Figures and Tables

Acknowledgements

I have always said I can provide advice to anyone who has kids the same age as mine or younger. Any older and it is a complete mystery. So along with my wonderful partner and soul mate, Jacquie (née Horler) we have had to learn along the way. And so it is to Jacquie and my three magnificent kids, Doug, Ben and Emily that I owe most gratitude for what I have learnt about decision making. Families are full of that thing we call life and living a full life means lots of challenges, lots of uncertainty. What they have taught me most is that making decisions from the heart means no regrets.

As you may expect, the family I grew up in taught me plenty about decision making. While we did not always agree, we have always laughed and we have stuck together. Thanks Mum (Gwyneth), Dad (Vince who passed a few years ago), my sister Leslie and my brother Brett. I owe so much to all of you, no words can do it justice.

Then there is my extended family on the Australian and the Canadian side of the Pacific. They are all wonderful people. They have taught me many things about life, relationships and of course decision making.

To all my friends – I am blessed with too many to thank individually, so thank you all for everything you have taught me and for being there for me and my family. Aussie mateship is quite tangible. All of my mates (and you know who you are) have a love of life. We give life a crack. Because of your friendship I was exposed to much more of the world, much more quickly than I would have otherwise. What comes with that is learning, sometimes the hard way, the benefits of thinking things through.

Thank you to the Thought Leaders' community. If it were not for this community this book almost certainly would not exist. It was a chance meeting in 2010 that led me to glance at an email that drew me to sign up for my first Thought Leaders course.

Matt Church, founder of Thought Leaders Global, taught me that I was not running a business, I was running a practice, just like a doctor or a lawyer. It changed how I viewed what I was doing and who I was doing it for. I began to thrive on further challenging myself to think differently, to think up new ways of approaching old problems, to find new ways of communicating a challenge or a solution, to simply think, to talk to people about what I had been thinking about and to help them deliver a solution to a new or an old problem. This book is a testament to the difference Matt has made to my and Jacquie's life. Thanks Matt.

Now I find myself in Thought Leaders Business School with Matt as spiritual leader, Pete Cook "the implementer" as CEO, an excellent group of mentors and a wonderful group of Thought Leader colleagues. It is a close-knit, diverse and above all inspiring community.

While I have met and been inspired by more than 100 Thought Leaders during the last two years, I can't name them all here. There are a special few though that I have great pleasure in thanking.

Scott Stein, one of authors of the original *Thought Leaders* book and long-term partner of Thought Leaders Global, has been my mentor these past two years. He has been instrumental in getting my headspace to the point where I love every part of my role as a Thought Leader. Thanks Scott, I owe you plenty.

To Dr Richard Hodge, thanks for believing in me and what I had to offer. Matt Lumsdaine thanks for being the first guinea pig for my decision model and thanks for making the decision you did. Dr Andrew Pratley thanks for collaborating with me. It has been fun, I have learnt much and I look forward to our future successes.

To my editor, Caroline Falls, thanks for what you were able to do with my work. It was great to click with you and have your experience guide me. To David Williams, my illustrator, thanks for your friendship and your wealth of talent.

My final thanks goes to my team. Paula Rival has been a wonderful addition to our team. Your energy and enthusiasm has been fantastic for us.

And to my business manager, Jacquie, my wife and the mother of my children. Yes, she has taken on the greatest challenge in the business world today. Working with your partner, in particular when that partner is me! Thank you for putting up with me, for picking me up when I was down and for inspiring me. I love working with you and I love you.

Bryan Whitefield

Preface

I am passionate about thinking things through as I have found it the single best way to get the most out of life with little or no regret. As a young adult I was good at thinking things through when it came to my social life. My enthusiastic, impatient friends would often jump early at an opportunity offered to attend a party or meet friends in a bar on a Saturday night. Not me. I would make sure I was aware of the options, I would consider who was going to be there, what kind of atmosphere it would be, what it might cost and then choose the option I felt would ensure we had the most fun-packed evening. Many times I was first harangued for my dithering and later lauded for my insight.

I have been confident for many years that it was wise to continue to explore and learn more about decision making. However, it was not until I read a book originally published in the 1940s called *Administrative Behaviour* by Herbert A. Simon that I became so convinced that improving decision-making skills and processes was the answer to overcoming so many challenges and for grasping so many opportunities. In his book, Simon explains that once the purpose of an organisation is established, all that remains is for management to influence decision making to ensure the most appropriate actions are taken by those within the organisation to fulfil the organisation's purpose. Simon goes on to explain that a perfect decision is one in which all possible consequences are foreseen. But, there is no such luxury in the real world. Not all consequences are foreseeable. With that uncertainty I felt there was a need for other methods to help us manage uncertainty and make great decisions.

I started my career as a chemical engineer after graduating from the University of Sydney. I chose chem-eng after a tour of the engineering department at an open day because it fascinated me the most. What fascinated me? Its complexity. The fact that I had little or no clue as to what was happening inside the lab-sized distillation column, made of glass so I could see the bubbling, the splashing and the fluids being drawn off by exit pipes at different heights to the column. I simply had to find out more.

Over my career as a chemical engineer I learnt that the chemical industry is complex. Consequently, the industry had devised ways of managing that complexity. They had ways of representing entire plants on paper using piping and instrument diagrams and they had chemistry for describing in simple terms what was happening inside a reactor. Despite the efforts of the industry, people still made mistakes and those mistakes were sometimes catastrophic. Many hundreds, and sometimes thousands, were killed in accidents. And this risk continues to this day.

The industry turned to risk management to manage the uncertainties and the complexities. It, along with other high-risk industries, was one of the leaders in developing methods for making decisions where there was a high degree of uncertainty. I learnt these skills and from the mid-1990s started to bring them to the even more complex world of business. Why is the business world more complex? Because of people. In the chemical industry, many of the decisions are bound by the laws of physics and chemistry. As I developed my business facilitation skills, I had more and more opportunity to help executives make some of the most important decisions for their organisations and of their careers. All the time I was learning about the art of decision making.

I read, I researched and I thought. Decision making is tough and the risks are well documented by the likes of Kahneman, Tversky, Thaler, Plous, Gigerenzer and more. But, to me something was missing from the literature and from the real world of decision making. In time, the missing piece of the puzzle became clear to me. I developed a simple model to manage the risk in decision making.

In this book I articulate for you the risk posed when you are making decisions and, most importantly, why that risk exists. I provide you with a simple model you can use any time of any day to help you manage the risk in your decision making. I provide you with additional tools to dig deeper when the stakes are higher, and I provide you with a methodology for improving the decision making of your entire organisation.

All you need to do is decide. Decide you want to be different; decide to make a difference and to manage the risk in your decision making and of those around you.

Bryan Whitefield

Introduction

I have spent my career identifying for my clients the problems with their current approach to their business and helping them work out what they should do about it. The problem, nine times out of 10, is that the decision had already been made and I was being asked to help them make their goals as achievable as possible. Over hundreds of workshops with executive teams, I have watched poor decisions confirmed as part of the key strategy on which the organisation depends. The strategy ends up with band-aids plastered all over it, or worse still, completely unravels, taking management back to the starting line.

What leads to the poor decisions? Well, do any of these personalities ring a bell for you?

First of all we have the tough, gruff leader who thinks almost everyone he or she meets is at best inferior, and more likely an idiot. Their opinion is the only one that matters and that is the end of it.

Then we have the nodding CEO. The one who politely nods as if he or she is hearing your advice and then, immediately after you have left the room, makes an edict that suits him or herself. Same result as the tough, gruff leader, just a nicer exterior.

What about the overly trusting leader? The one that places emphasis on respecting other people's views and who believes that people learn from their mistakes? The problem is that this type of leader tends to overestimate the talents of others and underestimate the need for themselves to do something about it.

One type I am very familiar with is the growth CEO. This type will talk about profitable growth but send signals that they want growth for growth's sake. On one occasion, before I started my practice, I had the pleasure of dining in my CEO's office with a new client that a unit of the business had just won over from a key competitor. When I got back to my desk and was talking to a colleague, the truth came out that we had undercut the market rate by more than 30 percent. An unsustainable rate. We were a laughing stock.

One of my least favourite types is the showman leader. The egotist who dresses up in the smart suits, drives the fancy car and maintains their position through "stakeholder management". They keep their focus on the board: explaining to them how the best decisions were their own and the poorer ideas were the ideas of others. All the time, never venturing into the real land of strategic decision making and strategy development.

And finally there is the protected-species leader. The one who seems to have very little clue about the position the organisation is in and who is lucky enough to have friends in the right places and a team that can cover for them.

If you have been around for any length of time, I am sure you are familiar with these personality types when it comes to leaders on executive teams. However, while I have encountered these types of leaders, the vast, overwhelming majority of leaders I have met – and have the privilege of calling my clients – are good people, and they are smart.

One of the early working titles of this book was "Think it Through". It was called that because of my lifelong frustration with seeing people make dumb mistakes because they didn't stop and think things through. Then, I realised that in fact many good and smart leaders, especially when it comes to strategic decisions and the formulation of smarter strategies, do stop and think things through. However, unfortunately the reality is that often when I came along to test their strategy with them and their team, it did not take long to find holes in their plans. Some very large holes; some smaller that were patchable at an unplanned cost. Obviously, my title needed to include the how-to concept as well.

So why do smart people struggle to develop smarter strategies? The answer is two-fold. The first is that strategic decision making and the formulation of smarter strategies are done within a large cloud of uncertainty. By their strategic nature they are bigger decisions with potentially wider ramifications, positive and negative. For example, how can we know the price of oil with certainty in 12 months' time? How can we know with certainty what a competitor is planning to launch in the next quarter? How can we know with certainty who will and won't be working for us in six months' time? How can we know with certainty the take up of a new product?

The second answer is that they lack a good process for making key strategic decisions. What is the norm for making key strategic decisions? Often, it goes as follows:

Strategic planning off-site

We have likely all been involved in strategic planning sessions and have ideas about what they involve. They usually go something like this:

- A day is set aside two months ahead of time and the invitations are sent out to the leadership team.
- About one month out an agenda comes out with topics and names beside each one.
- Individuals prepare their presentations.
- Someone takes care of logistics for the off-site meeting including the very important choice of a restaurant for dinner.
- The day arrives and starts with a pep talk. The agenda is confirmed and it is agreed how the outcomes of a session will be captured.
- The first presentation is engaging, runs a bit long and leaves you hanging as to what decision needs to be made. What was the question being asked?
- The second presentation goes over time as well and so the third presentation is started after a shortened morning tea. The presenter speeds through and hits you with a

recommendation you feel you have insufficient background understanding of to make an informed call. The decision is delayed until later in the day.

- Team building exercise.
- More presentations.
- Document actions and responsibilities.
- The wrap-up pep talk.

The end result is that you head back to work with all the problems you had before you went to the off-site session, plus now you have a list of new actions to undertake.

Strategy paper

The next step is to develop a strategy paper. A business case is presented. It has background information, a host of graphs and statistics, studies of the competition, and the all-important analysis done using the SWOT matrix – strengths, weaknesses, opportunities and threats. The decision seems pretty clear. So the team decides to approve it.

Six months later the strategy starts to unravel. People start coming out of the woodwork saying that they knew the strategy was doomed to fail. Why didn't they say anything at the time? Because they weren't asked.

Strategic plan

Just like the strategy paper, the strategic plan has plenty of background information, a host of graphs and statistics, competitor analysis and the SWOT matrix. There is also the vision statement, the strategic pillars, some strategic imperatives and a whole host of strategic initiatives. All wrapped up with a comprehensive list of key performance indicators, or KPIs, for each initiative, imperative and pillar.

The result? A plan that no one wants to wade through. A plan that people interpret for their area of the business as best they can, but one they can't be bothered to read through to understand what it all means. Reporting against the KPIs requires two people full-time for two weeks for each reporting period. And then, most of what is produced is not considered by management anyway.

I don't know how many books you have read on strategy and strategic decision making. As you would expect, I have read quite a few. The interesting observation that I have made is that while all of them provide insight and/or a set of tools to develop a smarter strategy, none of them address the one fundamental flaw in our strategic decision making. Not one of them provides a process to manage the underlying issue that there is risk in our decision-making processes. A management team may be using the latest tools out of Harvard Business School, London Business School or Wharton University or the tools from one of the big consulting firms such as McKinsey, Bain & Co or the Boston Consulting Group. That does not mean they will use them well, even if they are trained up in them. There is risk lurking in their decision making that needs to be managed.

In Part I of this book, I explain the extent of the opportunity you have as a strategic leader if you choose to improve your approach to decision making and the formulation of smarter strategies. I identify the three key elements of a strategic decision and why they pose a risk to your decision making. My aim is to convince you that uncertainty is the strategic leader's best friend. Conquer the uncertainty and you will have strategies that are smarter than those of any of your competitors.

In Part II, I focus in on the first key element of strategic decision making: your motivation behind the decision. Using real life examples, I help you explore how motivation determines mindset and that your mindset can be both a wonderful asset and a massive hindrance in formulating smarter strategies.

Part III explains the concept of doing what I call the "hard-smart" work. The second key element of decision making is to clarify your options before making the decision. In this part, I cover some of the dos and the don'ts. I ask you to consider alternative options and to think about outcomes on a continuum rather than at a fixed point. I ask you to put perceptions behind you and to get over phobias such as fear of paralysis by analysis.

Part IV addresses the third key element of strategic decision making and formulating smarter strategies – implementation. I spend a significant portion of the book talking about capability and the current lack of an accepted methodology in business to assess capability. The result: we overestimate capability and face problems down the track or we underestimate it and miss out on opportunities. Irrespective of your assessment of capability,

I show you that there is a pathway to cascading success, where you are rising out of the success of one initiative and into the path of another one. This is a pathway that you can take with creative leaders, talented teams and focused people.

Part V introduces my so-called MCI model for decision making. That's M for motivation, C for clarification and I for implementation. It's a simple model that you can use any time you wish to make a decision. The model is accompanied by a range of tools that will help you to identify and manage the risk in your decision making. I finish with the concept of identifying strategic potential and the need to match the type of strategy with the potential opportunity. The last section of Part V covers how you can apply what you have learned across your organisation.

At the end of the book I provide a quick tip sheet, comprising my 10 tips for strategic decision making and strategy formulation.

Throughout my career I have been on a journey to discover how best we can manage uncertainty. I want what we all want, to guide myself to make the best decisions I can make and then stay true to my heart and see them through. I am sure this book will make you stop and think the next time you recognise one of the risk factors in your decision making. I also hope that it will cause you to see the risk in the decision making of others and that it provides you with the tools you need to guide others. The more successful you become at that, the better for you and for those you lead.

Part I

For a strategic leader, uncertainty is your friend

Chapter 1

Houston, we have a problem

Landing a man on the moon in 1969 was one of humankind's greatest achievements, yet it had its problems along the way. Three astronauts died, it cost more money than originally projected and although NASA met the deadline that President Kennedy had set in 1961 to achieve this massive feat "by the end of the decade", it took longer than planned.

So what is a successful strategic decision? So many of our decisions seemed right at the time, however, often, with the benefit of our old friend Harry Hindsight, who shows up with a smug look on his face whenever things go wrong, the sheer stupidity of our decision is pointed out to us. It's not a great feeling is it?

Well, don't feel too bad about it, we all get things wrong from time to time, right?

If you answered yes to that question you are with the rest

of us humans. You, like I used to, have accepted mediocrity in strategic decision making.

While I might not be the greatest decision maker ever born (ever heard of me, seen me speaking at the United Nations or seen me accepting a Nobel Prize?) I do have a reputation for thinking things through. Maybe it is the Boy Scout in me, ingrained as a youth with the movement's motto "Be Prepared". Perhaps it was my enjoyment of the sciences at school where I learnt there was more to most things than meets the eye, or perhaps I was born this way? One thing I am certain of is that I like to get the most out of life and to get the most out of life you have to think things through, as much as time will allow, in order to make the best decision you can. That's the best path to a life with no regrets.

Our tendency to impulsiveness

While the no-regrets part of my life equation was in line with the thinking of my friends when we were in our teens and early twenties, the thinking-things-through part of the equation wasn't. You know, those years of impulsive behaviour, especially for young men, where stopping and thinking was something we did only after the fact on too many occasions. Often I would drive my friends crazy with my insistence to stop and think about the options. My friends would want to drop everything and take up the first offer for the next bit of fun and I would be heard saying, "Wait up, think it through. If we do that, we will most probably miss out on …"

In my 21st year I was at my peak when it came to assisting my friends on making the big decisions in order to get the most fun out of life. In Australia we have a tradition where we celebrate our 21st birthdays in a big way; some in a way that would challenge the wildest Hollywood party. So it was not uncommon to have two, three and sometimes more invitations to a 21st party on the same Saturday night. Think of the challenges. Who is the closest friend? Which is most likely to be the best party? How many can I go to in the one night?

Now living in a big city like Sydney, we had the added challenge of travelling significant distances between parties so the logistics were somewhat more complicated. In addition, this era was pre-mobile phones so we couldn't call from one party to the next to see which one was shaping up as the most fun. More than occasionally I was being thanked for the decision to go to "The best party ever!" or, for avoiding "The most boring party of my life!" as reported by others who chose differently to us.

While choosing the best party to go to when you were 21 was a big deal back then, life is of course much more serious and so incredibly uncertain. Stop for a second and think how much of life goes to plan. Think about what you thought you would be doing now, 10, 20 or even 30 years ago. Think where you thought you might be living, the people you might have been with, the work you might have been doing, the places you might have travelled to, the amount of money you might have had, the number of tragedies you might have seen, heard or experienced. Now grab a pencil (or pull up your favourite drawing app) and draw a circle. That circle is now a pie. Now dissect the pie into two pieces. One to represent how much of your life has gone per plan and the other how much of it has not. If you are anything like me, the as-per-plan piece is very much smaller than the not-to-plan piece.

So one of the pitfalls of wanting to think things through in order to make better decisions is that you can tie yourself up in knots thinking about what could happen, rather than making things happen.

Have a look at the diagram below and the quote from Christopher Simmons, associate vice president of federal relations at US-based Duke University. I love the quote. It tells me to embrace uncertainty. What I would add to it is to embrace uncertainty with the best tools available for managing uncertainty.

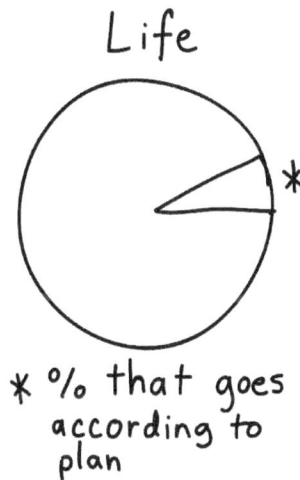

Don't be afraid to diverge from your 'plan'. Embrace ambiguity. The uncertain and what may appear high risk in relationships, jobs and life is usually very cool and worthwhile.

Source: *Duke Today*. Author: Christopher Simmons. Artist: Jonathan Lee.

The uncertainty paradox

We need to balance any decision we have made with that all too common occurrence when someone says "if only we knew then what we know now". So what we need to do is work out when we should stop and find out more information and think it through. Much easier said than done right? Take the example of John Key, Prime Minister of New Zealand, post the 2011 earthquake that destroyed many parts of Christchurch.

Christchurch is in the Canterbury region of the South Island of the country. New Zealand itself is part of a fault line. It is literally part of the boundary between the Pacific and Australian tectonic plates. On top of that, much of Christchurch is built on some of the worst possible soils you can have when it comes to earthquakes. The soil factor was well known prior to the Canterbury earthquakes of 2010 and 2011. In my role as risk adviser to the LAPP Fund, a local government mutual established in 1993 to finance damage from natural catastrophes to assets such as underground piping, I was in a meeting with a scientist from New Zealand's GNS Science following the first disaster and he mentioned that he and his colleagues were surprised more of Christchurch did not suffer from the earthquake phenomenon called liquefaction.

Liquefaction is the process where soft, sometimes wet, soils are shaken violently in an earthquake and the ground is seen to "boil". This causes the soil to lose its strength and any structure not sitting on piles, or pilings, embedded in rock become unstable. After the Christchurch earthquake large areas of the city were covered with a layer of thick sediment. It was such a problem that it inspired Sam Johnson, a 21-year-old student from the University of Canterbury in Christchurch, to start a Facebook page entitled "Student volunteer base for earthquake clean up", which later morphed into the Student Volunteer Army. Johnson literally created an army of students with shovels who helped remove the soil. In 2015, the Student Volunteer Army continues to help the Christchurch community in recovering from the earthquake, a process that will be ongoing for many more years. To give you a further idea of how important a role the student army played for what was a massive challenge, Johnson was awarded Young New Zealander of the Year in 2012.

The problem of soil deposited all over the city was one challenge, the damage that the liquefaction caused to buildings and infrastructure and the ultimate loss of life was far, far worse. No lives were lost in the September 2010 event, however, there was extensive damage with tales of close calls across the city, in particular from collapsing chimneys as people slept in the early hours of the morning when the earthquake struck. While touring Christchurch on behalf of the LAPP Fund some five months after the first earthquake and just 10 days before the second and more devastating earthquake, I was able to appreciate first-hand the scale of the damage, and the scale of the challenge facing the community. Not only was it the cracks in roads that were still apparent and the steel beams propping up damaged buildings on almost every street in the central business district, it was also the extent of damage to underground water and sewer systems. Five months after the event, the local council was still only part way through using CCTV cameras to identify the extent of damage to pipes, let alone being in a position to repair them. It was evident this work would go on for many years.

Because of this first-hand knowledge of the 2010 earthquake event, I was in the unenviable position of knowing how serious the second event was when I heard news of it. I was driving along Military Road, Mosman in Sydney returning from a morning workshop in the city. As I heard the first news reports depicting the scenes of collapsed buildings and pin-pointing the epicentre of the quake much closer to the city of Christchurch, my heart sank. I felt an ache right in the pit of my stomach, one we have all felt to one degree or another. It was not long before the reports tallied the number of deaths at more than 180 and the cost estimates to rebuild at more than NZ$10 billion. Over the next few weeks and months the ongoing widespread disruption to the social fabric of the city and the region became evident as families were forced to leave and planners, engineers and construction workers moved in.

In August 2014, the Christchurch Central Development Unit reported that more than 1,000 buildings had been levelled in the CBD. Of those, some 200 private-sector sites had been rebuilt or were underway. However, none of the major public buildings had been completed. A major piece of infrastructure to reignite the city, the CBD bus interchange was planned for completion by mid-2015 and inner-city residential living was scheduled to resume in 2016.

The conclusion one can draw from the story of Christchurch so far is that, just like so many other communities built on fault lines, cities built on the bends of massive rivers (like Brisbane, Australia) and major industrial precincts built on flood plains (like Thailand), it was simply built in the wrong place by people unaware of the potential of mother nature. Easy to say, isn't it?

Now consider the decisions facing the New Zealand Prime Minister, John Key, and his ministers and their advisers in the days following the February 2011 earthquake event. Key frequently reassured Cantabrians, including the people of Christchurch, that New Zealand would stand by them and that their city would be rebuilt.

In my experience of the phenomenon of disasters, the early estimates of the impact are grossly underestimated. I remember the first news report I heard of the Boxing Day Tsunami of 2004 in the Indian Ocean estimating more than 5,000 lives lost. I was shocked that so many people had died from a tidal wave, something I had some knowledge about because of my involvement with the LAPP Disaster Fund. Then the estimates started rising to 20,000 and then whole islands were thought to have been wiped out with tens of thousands of inhabitants lost. Final estimates of the toll reached well over 200,000.

In the case of Christchurch, the cost to rebuild was estimated at over NZ$10 billion within a few weeks. Current estimates, four years after the second event, have topped $40 billion.

Just last year I was speaking to a senior policy adviser in New Zealand's Department of the Prime Minister and he opined about the statements made by the Prime Minister in those early days following the second disaster and he wondered, "If we all knew then the likely cost, would we have been so keen to support a rebuild?"

The truth for New Zealand is that there are higher earthquake hazards to be concerned about. The nation's capital Wellington is also built on a massive fault line. I have often heard that if Wellington has "the big one", the city will be abandoned. I am not sure that anyone knows what that really means, nor can we imagine the challenges the population of New Zealand would face if a catastrophic event for Wellington came to pass.

My point? Decision making is difficult. In fact, at times it is mightily difficult. Think of the emotion that Key and his advisers were experiencing in the days following the earthquake. Think about how the desire to help the people of the Canterbury region must have been burning. On the other hand, think about how much money has been poured into the region to repair earthquake damages while others in New Zealand face the poverty line. Investment in other areas of the country may have developed a stronger New Zealand to support more of its people. Rebuilding Christchurch could be one of the biggest decisions ever made for New Zealand. The truth is we won't know for decades, perhaps a century. Therein lies a paradox. The only certainty is the uncertainty of our big, strategic decisions. The question is, what can or should we do about it?

The three key elements of decision making

The massive uncertainty facing Key, his cabinet and their advisers, highlights many of the difficulties about decision making. The first is the effect our emotions have on what motivates us around the decisions we need to make. The second is about the often incomplete information and the lack of clarity we have of the options we can choose from. And finally, once the decision is made, are we willing, ready and most importantly, able to see it through? Ask yourself how many great decisions were torpedoed by a distraction or the lack of commitment of key stakeholders?

The Christchurch example highlights the three key elements of strategic decision making that I focus on in this book: motivation, clarification and implementation. These are the elements that will help you deal with the fact that the only certainty is the uncertainty of our big, strategic decisions and help you to manage the risk in your decision making.

I have called my model the MCI model. I have focused on these particular elements for the reasons set out below:

Motivation because it creates strong emotions that can be used to enhance our decision making, or to block us from seeing reality. In the period moving from days to weeks and years, Key's motivations may have moved from strong concern for the emotional upheaval for Cantabrians to more of a political, or more of a pragmatic, view. So, not only do we need to be aware of how our motivations can affect our decision making, we also need to be aware of how our motivations will change over time.

Clarification because gut feel only works in certain circumstances, and it is misused by decision makers too often. Also, we tend to go straight to implementing the first and most obvious solution without considering the alternatives. Key stated the obvious and declared that the government would help rebuild Christchurch. In the aftermath, as costs soared, some have wondered if Christchurch should have been rebuilt, or if the money should have been spent on relocation to "firmer ground".

Implementation because we get distracted and don't stay focused until the decision is fully implemented, or because we have the uncanny ability to overestimate our capability in the first place, and don't accept changes are required. As the scale of the challenge and the price tag rose for Christchurch, Key and his advisers must have re-examined the nation's willingness, readiness and ability to see Christchurch rebuilt to its former glory.

In their book titled *Rework*, Jason Fried and David Heinemeier Hansson, the creators of the Basecamp project-management phenomenon, suggest that the worst possible time to make a detailed plan for a major initiative is at the beginning. That's when we know the least!

This means that thinking of a decision as a singularity, singular in time and outcome, is a very big mistake. A more holistic approach is required.

Chapter 2

Your decisions define you

Ultimately your decisions define you. Think about people you know. Those who are no longer with us due to that one fateful decision; those who live a very different life to the one you imagined they would lead. Think about famous people such as India's Mahatma Gandhi, South Africa's Nelson Mandela and Myanmar's Aung San Suu Kyi. Think of those infamous people from Germany's Adolf Hitler to Iraq's Saddam Hussein. You have an image of each of them in your mind that is there because of the decisions they took.

What about sports people, politicians and business leaders that are more familiar to you? How are they defined?

Let's look at sports people. There are so many positive examples of sports people defined for their swerve, their nerve, their speed, their agility, their ability to make the right split-second call on a play. However, there are also those defined by their impulsive behaviour. Think Mike Tyson, John McEnroe and Luis Suarez. Suarez is a world-renowned, elite soccer player from Uruguay who played for European powerhouses Liverpool and Barcelona. In the 2014 FIFA World Cup he bit his Italian opponent Giorgio Chiellini. Suarez had been banned for biting twice before. Defined.

Now let's turn to politics and take a look at John Hewson. Hewson was Liberal opposition leader in the Australian parliament when he went into a national election up against the formidable Labor leader Paul Keating in 1993. In what some may say is familiar territory, Australia's balance sheet had been weakened during the successful reign of Labor's Bob Hawke as prime minister since 1983. Recognising the concern of the community as the economic climate deteriorated in the early 1990s, Hewson launched "Fightback" – an economic policy looking to raise revenue, cut costs and fix the spending deficit in a bid to repair the balance sheet of the country. But Hewson had not fully reckoned on the ability of Keating to paint a picture of unnecessary hardship for the poor and for the middle class that Fightback would bring. Keating was lauded far and wide for his oratory skills and here they came to the fore.

The item that proved the most contentious issue of the ensuing 1993-election campaign was the conservative party's plan to introduce a broad-ranging goods-and-services tax, or GST. Who can forget the interview where Hewson fumbled through his response when asked to explain how the GST applied to a birthday cake? Earlier, Hewson had listened to criticism about how the GST would unfairly impact the less well-off and had agreed the tax should not apply to fresh food. This introduced all kinds of complexities, highlighted by the birthday-cake interview. At the end of the day Fightback was coined "the longest suicide note in history"!

How is Hewson defined? By his decision to create the Fightback policy and publish it well in advance of the election. Ever since, opposition parties have created very small targets up until election campaigns are in full swing. Irrespective of the outcome, one question that can never be answered is: Was Hewson's decision to publish Fightback the wrong decision or, was the problem his implementation of the decision?

MCI – motivation, clarification and implementation are the cornerstones of great decision making. Implementation requires the commitment to see it through. Hewson could see how effective Keating was with his messaging, Keating was frightening people about the cost of food, so Hewson decided to make the change to the policy to exclude fresh food. By doing so he introduced two things into the equation in his election fight. One was complexity in the policy that even he found hard to explain. The other was doubt about the strength of his convictions, his willingness to see things through.

While Hewson was mainly defined by that one big decision to publish Fightback, the political stage is an important example of how we can make one unpopular or bad decision and still come up smelling like roses. After all, anyone can make a mistake, right?

US President Bill Clinton oversaw a strong economy, including a budget surplus which was the first in decades and two more after that. He executed the North American Free Trade Agreement and a new trade agreement with China. He was involved in brokering peace in Bosnia and Northern Ireland; the latter being no mean feat given the length of the dispute and how well the negotiated peace has lasted. Clinton also tried to initiate universal health care but was blocked by congress. It was another 20 years before Barrack Obama became president and took on the same battle, and won.

While you have been reading you have probably been thinking about that infamous event of Clinton's presidency. Can you hear those words now? "I did not have sexual relations with that woman!" During his presidency and as a married man, he did have sex with that 23-year-old woman, Monica Lewinsky. Yet Clinton's many great decisions while president leave him being judged favourably by history. The balance of his decisions defined him. Everyone is allowed to make a mistake it seems.

How about a business example. Try Mark Zuckerberg of Facebook. What a star right? Except there is still that nagging feeling he may have cheated, as is played out in the movie *The Social Network*. While it is very difficult to know the truth, and the truth often lies somewhere between two people's memories of the events, the facts are Facebook did settle more than one lawsuit with people claiming they had the initial concept. But then again, by which value system am I judging Zuckerberg? My own of course. Others will see Zuckerberg as simply smart, a good business man. Others will forgive him completely, thinking, "He was young, ambitious. Young men are quite self-centred, he would not have been listening too clearly," or, "He was an IT geek. Geeks are not so hot on the emotional intelligence side of things."

So, not only do our decisions define us, these examples are also a reminder of how complex decision making can be. These examples show clearly we need to understand what motivates us, we need to understand the potential consequences of our decisions, and we need to be able to see them through.

In his book *Thinking Fast and Slow*, acclaimed behavioural psychologist Daniel Kahneman describes the dual phenomenon of "duration neglect" and the "peak-end rule", which when combined "cause a bias that favours a short period of intense joy over a long period of moderate happiness" with a mirror image where we are much more concerned about a short, but intense, bad experience than we are about a prolonged period of milder, poorer experience. That is why politicians put out the painful policies in the early period of their term in office and roll out the "pork barrel" to sweeten people up at the end of their term. They are gambling that the pain felt from the tough policies will either result in a good outcome for which they will later be applauded or will be forgotten about by the time of the next election as people feel at least warm towards what is now on offer.

On a final note about decisions defining the person, you should also be thinking about how you can't make all the decisions. Think of the Uruguayan football manager and his star player Luis Suarez. The manager had a plan and Suarez didn't follow the plan. The football-loving nation of Uruguay, with a population of more than three million went into shock, then anger and finally mourning as they saw their hopes of victory dashed when Suarez was thrown out of the 2014 World Cup for biting. So it is not only your decisions you need to worry about, you need to worry about everyone else's decisions as well!

Have you thought about the value of a decision?

Before you can adequately identify the value of a decision, you need to get your head around valuing intangibles. I know, I know, it is difficult, however, we do have some very clear examples. One of the most famous and clear is the story of Facebook.

On May 18, 2012 Mark Zuckerberg's Facebook was publicly listed for trading on the US stock exchange with a market valuation in the vicinity of US$100 billion dollars. Impressive wasn't it? In fact, it was incredibly impressive as it was based on annualised earnings in the vicinity of US$500 million. By February 19, 2014, Facebook's market capitalisation was of the order of US$170 billion when 2013 earnings were around US$2 billion. According to the NASDAQ, Facebook's 2013 price-earnings ratio was about 129[1], compared with a prevailing PE average of about 20 for technology stocks.

---

1   Price/earnings ratio is given by dividing the last sale price by the average EPS (earnings per share) estimate for the specified fiscal time period. From: http://www.nasdaq.com/symbol/fb/pe-ratio#ixzz3Q67j6lwv

That is, some way, somehow, investors figured that Facebook had the potential to grow its earnings to the extent it could return to shareholders $129 for $1 invested now. Put it another way, the "market" felt that Zuckerberg, the board and management and staff could collectively make the right decisions to justify their investment in the company. There were no hard assets, no guaranteed revenue streams, there was simply a phenomenon that positioned Facebook in a new market segment just like Amazon and Google had done. Investors believed that somehow the team, with all that intellectual capital, would work out how to make future revenue streams many, many times higher.

So, how important is a decision and how does the value of one big decision, say made by you, compare with the value of decisions made by others later in a project? Let's think about the decision to expand capacity of an existing manufacturing process. Let's assume that to do this it will cost in the order of $100 million and will take six to nine months from decision time until the first product from the expanded facility is being shipped to market. The first decision, to expand the plant or not, is obviously the biggest one. However, once the decision is made, there will be many thousands of decisions being made by staff, contractors and suppliers before the plant is in full production. There will be decisions about technology and about which supplier to use. There will be decisions about the timing of purchases and modes of transport. There will be decisions about hiring additional plant operators and how to best train them. Are you getting the same feeling that I am getting? The size and the importance of decisions is reducing over time, however, their numbers are increasing as in the figure below, the decision value curve.

DECISION VALUE CURVE

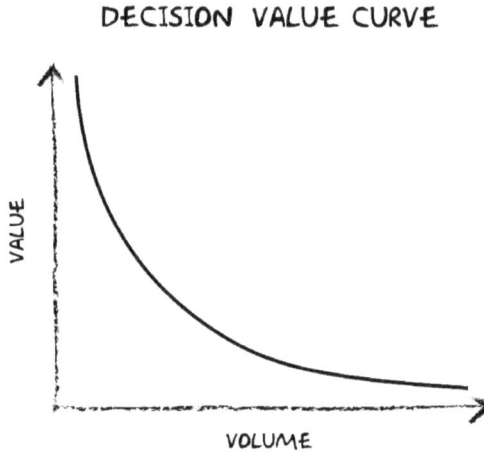

If you are a bit of a mathematician, you will recognise the curve as an inverse exponential curve. The area under the curve for any particular segment of the curve depicts the value of a decision or decisions. These types of curves indicate a rapid rate of change along the vertical axis (the value axis) as you move along the horizontal access (the volume of decisions), that is towards the tail of the curve. What it means is that one or two decisions at the beginning of the curve, which have a huge potential value, have exactly the same value as the thousands of decisions represented by the tail of the curve.

What does this mean for you? It means you had better get the big, early decisions as right as possible. However, it also means you had better have all your people making good decisions along the way, given the sheer volume of them being made. One poor choice can set a project back a month, or render a desired functional outcome no longer possible. So this is not just about you getting your decision making right or you making sure the executives get it right, it is about ensuring all of your people have the wherewithal to make great decisions. The problem is, they all have the hidden risks in their decision making as you do in yours.

Given the value of decisions across the enterprise, perhaps you should take a feather out of the hat of George Kirkland from Chevron. He calls himself a "Decision Executive" and is passionate about Chevron's decision-analysis process. The process was used for the Gorgon LNG project in Australia's north west. Given the value of the project was around US$40 billion, you bet Chevron wanted to get the initial investment decision right. I have no doubt that the process Chevron uses is a good one and helps ensure they make better investment decisions of this nature.

The next question is, is that decision-making process appropriate for the duration of the project? The answer of course is "no". Once the analysis was done and the decision had been made, Chevron would have had to turn its attention to project management and the influencing of the decisions of the thousands of managers, engineers, supervisors and the individuals working on the ground assembling the plant; the implementation segment of strategic leadership.

How good are you at decision making?

If you are a confident person, someone who has reached senior management or built a successful business, you will probably be of the view that your decision making is pretty good. Let's face it, you have made it to where you are while others haven't. The unspoken aspect of your decision-making skills is that there is still plenty of room for improvement. Have a think about the last five or 10 significant decisions you made. Here is a list of five common decisions to get you thinking:

- Terminated someone's employment.
- Invested in a new product or market.
- Upgraded or downgraded premises.
- Shifted strategic focus, for example, more growth orientated, or to build sustainability.
- Entered into an outsourcing arrangement.

While each one of these significant decisions may be great decisions, way too often they are in response to earlier poor decisions. Take the first one. Why did you need to terminate the person's employment? Did you hire the wrong person? Fail to develop their skills and all round capability? Did you not foresee the type of skills and capability you would need for the future? Is your business not running so well? Or, what about number four: the shift in strategic focus? If you have been on a singularly upward journey of success and this decision is simply to keep it that way then great, good on you. For many of us less capable folks, though, it is more likely in response to something that is not working so well. It is recognition that our best decisions often are not great forever because the world is a fast-changing one.

In bygone years you could become a shoe manufacturer, build a factory, get your costs under control, adapt to the change in fashions and expand capacity and sales channels with quite clear pathways. Before you knew it you were retiring or handing the business over to your successors. Nowadays fashions change every season and quick fads come with a celebrity's appearance at a dinner, on a talk show or from a tweet. With the advances in technology, shoes can now be made from many different materials with all kinds of different comfort or fashion aids. Throw in globalisation and you have to worry big time about supply-chain and cost management. How many new businesses last more than 10 years nowadays? How many mega businesses last a generation?

I think we all agree the world is a more complex place than ever before and consequently decision making faces more uncertainty than ever before. Ipso facto, decision making is simply harder. However, let me introduce you to a few bits of research that will help you establish a baseline for improving your decision making. All you need to do is decide if you are better than average, or not, and by how much.

Let's start with simple decisions. There is a field of engineering broadly encapsulated under the heading of "reliability". Some of its strongest growth was born out of disasters like the Union Carbide lethal chemical leak in Bhopal, India in 1984, the Piper Alpha oil platform fire in 1988, the Exxon Valdez oil tanker grounding in 1989, the Texas City BP oil refinery explosion in 2005, BP's Deepwater Horizon oil spill in 2010, New Zealand's Pike River mine explosion the same year, and the Fukushima nuclear meltdown following the impact of a tsunami in 2011. The reliability engineering profession in the latter half of the last century spent massive resources globally analysing systems failures. One of their greatest challenges was to try and quantify what is generally referred to in the industry as the "human-error rate". That is, when did someone make a decision that with the benefit of Harry Hindsight proved to be the wrong one?

The research and the published findings are intriguing and have led to new methods in the design of safety systems for high risk environments such as found in chemical plants, air travel and rail operations. Here are a few statistics for you from the so-called "human error assessment and reduction technique" developed by J.C. Williams.[2]

Table 1: Human error rates

Decision	Probability of error
Task that is unfamiliar, needs to be performed at speed, no idea of outcome	0.55
Complex task requiring high level of comprehension and skill	0.16
Routine, highly practised, rapid task involving relatively low level of skill	0.02
Totally familiar task, performed several times per hour, well motivated, highly trained staff, time to correct errors	0.0004

2   Smith, David J (2011). *Reliability,Maintainability and Risk*, 8th ed., Butterworth-Heinemann, Oxford U.K.

As you can see in Table 1 above, there is a very broad range of dependability of decision making even at the task level. And task-level decision making is much simpler than the average business decision you will be making this week.

Williams's methodology also uses modifying factors that are applied as multiples. It is well recognised that our decision making is influenced by a range of factors from our training and experience and the emotions one is feeling at a particular time. Indeed, there's also a strong belief that two heads are better than one. Table 2 below shows some of Williams's modifying factors and the proposed multiplying factor.

Table 2: Human error modifying factors

Error producing condition	Multiplying factor
Unfamiliar with infrequent and important situation	×17
Need to learn an opposing philosophy	x6
Newly qualified	x3
Little or no independent checks	x3
Incentive to use more dangerous approaches	x2
Emotional stress	X1.3

While you are right in thinking much of this research and analysis is based on decision making about manual tasks, not the type of business decisions you make on a regular basis, I think you can appreciate the times when you are more likely to get a decision right as opposed to when your decision making is most at risk. Your level of knowledge and understanding of the decision, though, is the most important one. The two tables above provide stark evidence for this.

A massive opportunity

Now to evidence from business of the quality of our strategic decision making. First to a survey of executives by consulting firm McKinsey & Co. As reported in an article by Dan Lovallo and Olivier Sibony[3] a 2009 survey of more than 2,200 executives showed that "only 28 percent said that the quality of strategic decisions in their companies was generally good, 60 percent thought that bad decisions were about as frequent as good ones, and the remaining 12 percent thought good decisions were altogether infrequent". Can I suggest that these figures speak for themselves? After all, McKinsey is a well-respected global consulting firm running global surveys.

Better than a survey, however, is the work of Paul C. Nutt. In his book *Why Decisions Fail*[4] Nutt unpacks decades of research into 400 decisions made by managers of organisations from a broad range of industries and from many countries. Many are household names in the US and worldwide, like AT&T, Disney and Ford. Nutt's criteria for judging a successful decision was whether the decision was "put to use" and that such use had to be sustained over at least two years. While

3 Lovallo D. & Sibony O. *McKinsey Quarterly*: "The Case for Behavioural Strategy," March 2010.

4 Nutt, Paul C (2002). *Why Decisions Fail: Avoiding the Blunders and Traps That Lead to Debacles*, Berrett-Koehler Publishers, San Francisco, CA.

any number of arguments could be made for a different set of criteria, Nutt's criteria is tough but reasonable given that these are strategic decisions.

Nutt's findings were that more than half of management decisions fail. That is a staggering amount given the time, money and will put into them. However, taking into account the statistics from the reliability engineers and the complexity of decision making, no one should be surprised.

I put these statistics, without the background on Nutt's criteria, to a police commissioner here in Australia and he argued that he felt that he and his team got the vast majority of the big decisions right. However, he followed up with a comment about the challenge of implementation, the stage that is required to ensure any decision is followed through. As you will find later in this book, I don't accept poor implementation as an excuse for non-delivery on a good decision. Obviously neither did Nutt, given his two-year horizon. The decision must take into account the challenge of implementation, which needs to be designed into the decision-making process.

Not convinced yet? Let's go to some statistics provided in a *Harvard Business Review* article written by Dan Lovallo and Daniel Kahneman. In their article titled "Delusions of Success: How Optimism Undermines Executives' Decisions"[5] they state:

---

5 Kahneman, Daniel & Dan Lovallo (2003). "Delusions of Success: How Optimism Undermines Executives' Decisions." *Harvard Business Review*, pp. 1-10.

More than 70 percent of new manufacturing plants in North America, for example, close within their first decade of operation. Approximately three-quarters of mergers and acquisitions never pay off – the acquiring firm's shareholders lose more than the acquired firm's shareholders gain. And efforts to enter new markets fare no better; the vast majority end up being abandoned within a few years.

While I have provided evidence of the difficulty of decision making at the task level and at the strategic level, I assume you are wondering about the decisions made in between. Well, I also have some evidence of the quality of decision making at more of a middle management level. I conducted a survey of members of the CPA/CSA Risk Discussion Group in Sydney in 2013. The survey was aimed at identifying, prior to a seminar I was due to deliver to the group of certified public accountants and company secretaries, what were the major causes of project failure. As most medium to large organisations are usually running hundreds or even thousands of projects, not all of them would be strategic ones, in fact many would be business as usual (BAU) ones, while others are part of implementation of a higher-level strategy. The survey results provide some insight into the quality of middle-management decision making.

The survey showed that 63 percent of participants indicated that more than four out of five projects do not fail. On this measure, middle management is looking good. We can imagine that BAU projects have a lot more certainty about them than larger strategic decisions. We can also assume that some of the newer projects, where we don't have so much experience, will be more likely to fall into the 20 percent of unsuccessful projects.

On the other hand, only 15 percent of survey participants felt that more than 80 percent of projects were highly successful. When the bar was dropped to "60 percent of projects are highly successful", the agreement rate rose to 30 percent. For me, this indicates what I have always contended, that although there are plenty of projects that are not an outright failure, there are plenty that have mediocre outcomes. In fact, in my experience, an acceptance of mediocrity and an acceptance that projects (and decision making) are difficult are the norm in the vast majority of organisations. Certainly, that's the case in the hundreds that I have worked with.

Following the risk discussion-group session, I wrote a paper to summarise the results and my views on what they meant for project management. I headlined the paper: "Why could we land a man on the moon in 1969 yet in 2013 we struggle to get a moderate sized IT project delivered successfully? – An acceptance of mediocrity?"

Now, I admit this relatively small survey of a group of Sydney-based, mostly middle managers, is by no means as rigorous as Nutt's, however, it does reinforce what the task-based and strategy-based data are telling us.

There is a mammoth opportunity for you to improve your decision making and those at all levels of your organisation. While the most important decisions are made at the top, each decision is followed by thousands of decisions over the coming weeks, months and years which also need to be right far more often than wrong. Given your decision making defines you, it is an opportunity you can't afford to miss.

Chapter 3

Management, we have a problem

There can be no doubt with this weight of evidence across organisations that we have a problem with making good decisions and with accepting mediocre outcomes. The funny thing is, we continue to accept it as the norm. Meanwhile, we provide plenty of material for comic strips like *Dilbert* and comedy shows such as *The Office* and, more recently in Australia, *Utopia* (called *Dreamland* in the UK and US).

Here, the writers all use satire to point out the absurdity and sometimes the stupidity that occurs in business and government decision making. I was at a conference dinner in late 2014 and three of us were discussing *Utopia*. One of the three of us was from government, which is *Utopia*'s setting. My government colleague said: "I was watching it just last week. I had just come back from a two-day off-site with the executive team. I thought, 'These guys must have been taping us'!"

Similarly, I was lunching with a colleague recently who is a senior finance executive with a long career in large corporations. We were discussing me writing this book and he was saying *The Office* was his favourite show. He said he wanted to write a humorous book on similar themes he had seen in decision making over his career. His concern for my success with this book was that he didn't think anyone recognised the problem. At least not sufficiently well enough to do anything about it.

I told him I liked a challenge and that I felt it was time for someone like me to unveil the elephant in the room. The elephant in the room is the thing that is obviously there, but no one sees it. The challenge is for strategic leaders to decide to do something about the risk in their decision making.

It's like Ground Hog Day

I assume that you started reading this book because you knew your strategic decision making, or your team's, could and should improve. Hopefully, by now, with me asking you to think about your decision making and the decision making you see around you, together with the research I have referred to so far, you are convinced there is room for improvement. You know we all have a tendency to make assumptions and take short cuts so we don't always make the best decisions. You know we have all had the experience of wishing we could take back a decision.

If we actually started to focus on improving our decision

making we could ultimately live much closer to our dream world than being caught in the rat race we live in today.

Have you seen the movie *Groundhog Day*? In the movie, US comedian Bill Murray plays the part of Phil Connors, a weatherman reporting the Groundhog Day ceremony in Punxsutawney, Pennsylvania. The celebrated day is a US tradition where an animal known as a groundhog is used to "predict" the length of winter. If it pops out of the hole and stays out, winter is ending soon. If it pops back in, it will be a long winter. That, however, is not the important point; the saying "It's like Groundhog Day" is referring to experiencing the same, generally negative thing, again and again and again.

In the movie, Phil gets caught in a time loop where he keeps waking up at 6 a.m. on Groundhog Day and reliving the same day, over and over and over again. The plot involves a series of hilarious mischievous events created by Phil because he knows what is going to happen throughout the day. He eventually grows tired of it. Soon he falls for the beautiful news producer Rita Hanson (Andie MacDowell). She, though, does not fall for him.

Eventually, after making the same mistake time and time again as he tries to manipulate her to find out what she likes and doesn't like, Phil turns over a new leaf and decides he wants to be a good man and help others. Eventually he wins Rita's heart because of who he becomes. He broke the cycle.

The saying, "It's like Groundhog Day", reminds me of another saying: "You never make the same mistake twice." If you believe that, you have never lived. You may never have made the same gargantuan mistake twice because it hurt so bad, however, we all make smaller mistakes time and time again. We are living like Phil Connors in *Groundhog Day*. We are making the same mistakes over and over and over. The question is, what are we willing to do to break out of our time loop?

What are you willing to do? Do you have a fixed mindset or a growth mindset? Carol S. Dweck, in her book *Mindset*, writes that with a fixed mindset, you believe that your basic abilities are fixed; if you believe your basic abilities can be developed through retraining, you have a growth mindset. Do you simply believe decision making is difficult for everyone and that we all make mistakes? Do you believe our series of poor decisions is a fact of life? Or do you believe there are things to learn and that we can improve?

Caught in the rat race

How are things in your world right now? Things under control. Not too many staffing issues, revenue up nicely on last year, no one has blown their budget by much so far this year, you are managing the flow of information coming your way quite nicely and, oh, your inbox is empty at the end of each day, right?

We both know the reality is quite different. This fast paced, complex world is becoming tougher and tougher to manage day-to-day, month-to-month, quarter-to-quarter and year-to-year. And therein lies a secret to your problems. How are you managing your decision making day-to-day, month-to-month, quarter-to-quarter and year-to-year?

Let me paint an ugly picture for you. One you are likely to see yourself in the midst of.

Daily – While you are considering the news that a competitor has just announced a price reduction of 30 percent on your key product, a team leader walks through the door declaring loudly that a staffing issue is evidence of a culture problem that has developed in the past six months.

That is, while you are considering an important, strategic decision that needs to be addressed in the short term, other problems get in your way. Often problems that also require immediate attention and other times problems that need a much longer-term solution.

Monthly and Quarterly – The numbers for the past month are trending down, just as they had in the previous month. It is fourth quarter. If you don't turn around the numbers in the next month, the year-end bonuses for staff and your management will be in jeopardy. You are getting pressure from both management and staff. You are not a panic merchant, you have seen this before and the pipeline looks like it will deliver. You are expected to be a leader and you soldier on.

You have set up your organisation around short-term reward. This drives short-term thinking.

Yearly – Before anyone knows it, the request for next year's annual plan and budget are being asked for. Management hastily throw together a strategic off-site. The agenda is not well thought through, people come ill-prepared, the first few sessions run over time, you head back to the office with more things to do and you still have every other problem you had before you left.

That is, you don't stop to break the cycle. You push on through the stress and strain year on year. You are tough. You are a leader.

Strategic leaders break the cycle. They make sure the organisation stops long enough to think through the issues at appropriate time intervals while investing in an appropriate level of resources using an appropriate process. That could be daily, monthly, quarterly, annually and longer-term depending on the rate of change in their organisation. Take the military for example. In the midst of a war, strategic decisions are being made daily. In peace time, the more corporate-style monthly, quarterly and annual planning and reporting occurs. However, they also plan for the much longer-term to address the need to prepare for future threats and the long lead time on delivering often large and technologically ground-breaking military capability. The military has five-, 15- and 30-year plans.

Over what time frames do you review your strategy? What processes do you use to review your decisions?

Solutions abound

Decision making is something we are doing almost every second of our waking moments and there are many good sources of written material on the topic of good, versus bad, decision making. In fact, so much has been written about decision making you would be excused for being confused. Let's take a look at the lay of the land from a range of researchers and authors.

I have already mentioned the 2009 McKinsey Global Survey of decision makers.[6] The survey asked respondents to concentrate on one recent decision and asked if it was successful or not. It then asked them to agree or disagree with a range of statements about their decision-making process. In reporting on the results, McKinsey identified the various practices that good performers did more of than did poor performers. For example, McKinsey identified that good performers were much more likely to base decision making on a good balance of financial and strategic targets, and a balance of short- versus long-term thinking. They also identified a key factor was the clarity of understanding of an organisation's capabilities to implement. However, it still remained that even for companies that were poor performers, many of them were trying to undertake most of the better practices. One could be excused for thinking that something may be missing, even if you believe that making decisions on complex choices is tough.

Let's take a look at another consulting firm which conducts regular and serious research, Bain & Company. Bain & Co maintains a "high performers" database of 365 companies. In an

---

6 *Flaws in strategic decision making: McKinsey Global Survey Results*, McKinsey & Company Insights and Publications, 2009

analysis of the data, Paul Rogers and Marcia Blenko[7] report on the differences between the 57 top performers and the rest of the pack of high performers when it comes to decision making. They focus on five elements; leadership, accountability, people, execution and culture. They highlight themes like "clear vision", being "focused on what matters", "superior capabilities" and a "high-performance culture". Anything missing in your mind? Where's "excellent decision making"?

Let's move to some academic research. I have already referred to Paul Nutt's research into why decisions fail. Let's look a little further into the underlying causes he identifies for failed decisions.

At a high level, Nutt speaks of poor decision practices, over-commitment, or premature commitments and simply putting your effort in the wrong place, particularly in terms of time and money. As he digs deeper, he writes of the need to be aware of social and political forces, the need for innovation, the pitfall of unethical practices and the role of incentives in driving good and bad decision making. In considering the implementation of our decisions, Nutt recognises the challenges of change management and why and how people resist change and the need for the decision-making process to deal with change. In fact, Nutt has so many underlying causes and accompanying

---

7   http://www.bain.com/bainweb/PDFs/cms/Marketing/Decision-driven%20 organization.pdf, Blenko, Marcia W., Michael C. Mankins and Paul Rogers (2010). "The decision-driven organization." *Harvard Business Review* 88 (6). pp. 54-62.

requisite good practices, the whole decision-making process becomes not just daunting, it becomes nigh on impossible. It is no wonder we accept a 50 percent success rate for our decisions. Why then don't we just toss a coin?

In his doctoral thesis on executive decision making, Christopher Stephenson provides a strong body of evidence that the decision-making process of an organisation is a key factor behind poor decisions. He discusses cognitive factors, decision-making method and behavioural factors. Stephenson identifies strategic alignment as being at least as important when applying the process and breaks this down further to organisational alignment and motivational alignment.[8] In his reporting on his research, he lists scores of reasons given by research participants as to why good decisions aren't always made. They included transparency, diversity, data, mutual respect, emotion and even narcissistic behaviour. More great concepts here; maybe some overlap, and definitely some new things to worry about if you are trying to improve your decision making.

In *Decisive*, academics Chip and Dan Heath, explore the vagaries of our psychological biases. For them there are four biases that need to be dealt with: narrow framing, confirmation bias, the effect of short-term emotion on decisions, and the tendency to be over-confident. They offer a simple process they

---

8 Stephenson, CB (2012). "What causes top management teams to make poor strategic decisions?" Doctor of Business Administration (DBA) dissertation, Southern Cross University, Lismore, NSW, p. 21. Also at, http://epubs.scu.edu.au/theses/280/

call WRAP, which stands for widen (your options), reality (test your assumptions), attain (some distance) and prepare (to be wrong). It's simple and they provide good guidance on how to apply the process. Still, from my point of view, something is missing.

Then there is the 2009 best-seller *Nudge* by Richard Thaler and Cass Sunstein. If you were not concerned about the complexity of decision making before, then *Nudge* should push you over the edge. In their book, Thaler and Sunstein describe the role of a "choice architect", someone who can frame a choice for people to the advantage of themselves or the people making the choice. They provide convincing evidence from years of research, referencing many brilliant works on choice that preceded their book. Each shows how you can design a choice to take advantage of our extremely fickle minds. If you get your design right you can influence most people to make the decision you want. In considering the role of a choice architect, Thaler and Sunstein suggest, "A good rule of thumb is to assume that 'everything matters'."[9] So, there you have it, everything matters when choosing and decision making is about killing off choices until you are left with the preferred option. If everything matters and uncertainty abounds, decision making is highly complex and we have a tough road ahead to improve our decision making.

---

9 Thaler, Richard H. & Sunstein, Cass R., *Nudge: Improving Decisions about Health, Wealth and Happiness* (2012), Penguin Books, London.

I'll finish with a slight detour from academia to a book written by an experienced decision-making business executive, David Goldsmith. In *Problem Solved*[10], Goldsmith writes of the need to ensure that you have a sound definition of the problem so that you are making decisions about the right problem, that is, you are asking the right question.

Given all the analysis of decision making, all the perceptions, assumptions and theories about decision making and the fact that mediocre, strategic decision making persists, one has to wonder if the right question about what is the essence of good decision making is even being asked.

---

10 Goldsmith, David (2014). *Problem solved: the secrets of decision making and problem solving*, Goldsmith Publishing, Chicago.

Chapter 4

The solution is right there within us

One man has made a lifetime of study into judgement and decision making in the hope of improving the lives of others. In fact, I have already mentioned him, Daniel Kahneman, and his most recent book, *Thinking Fast or Slow*. In his introduction, Kahneman explains that his aim with the book is to improve our ability to identify good and bad decision making by others, to provide a language that describes what we see to enable conversations that will help us learn the possible interventions that can either improve our decision making, or at least limit the downside.

The premise of his book is that we necessarily have an approach to making decisions when we have either limited time or the decision is of less importance, and that we have a different approach when we have bigger decisions to make and more time to think about them. The former is fast thinking and the latter is slow, more analytical thinking. Kahneman suggests the trick to good decision making is to find ways to recognise when you are thinking fast, when in fact it is a time for you to be thinking slow. As I said, he provides a raft of language to help describe the fast thinking we often do and he provides some language for thought processes to help trigger a shift into slow thinking.

Reading the works of Kahneman and the works of others from the fields of psychology and behavioural economics such as those mentioned from the Heaths, Nutt, Thaler and others including Gerd Gigerenzer, Scott Plous, and Sheena Iyengar has been cathartic for me. It emphasised that despite all the research and the insight provided in a broad range of sources, despite what is taught in schools and universities, despite what is readily available to all decision makers, decision making is still, at best, mediocre when it comes to the more complex decisions of business. What can and should we do to fix this?

The hidden risk

All of the authors and consulting firms I've mentioned so far have made suggestions on how to improve decision making. For example, Stephenson contends that the failure of top-level decisions is caused by "weak decision ecosystems" which are further eroded by the "political" tactics of executives who are full of self-interest.[11] His proposed decision model is strong on process, including

---

11 Stephenson, C.B. (2012). "What causes top management teams to make poor strategic decisions?" Doctor of Business Administration (DBA) dissertation, Southern Cross University, Lismore, NSW, Australia, p.18.

addressing behavioural factors while aiming for organisational and motivational alignment. The Heaths offer a process they call WRAP while Kahneman offers the clever "Thinking Fast and Slow". Indeed, without doubt we need a process.

The funny thing, is that the process we need is already within us. It is something we have been doing instinctively throughout our evolution. However, we are learning how to do it better. It is a process that is designed to learn from all the hard thinking of decision-making researchers, one that is designed to work with the complexity of our world, one that is ready built for the fact that the certainty is uncertainty. It is the process we use to assess and deal with risk. Our natural decision-making processes are fraught with risk. Why not manage the risk in our decision making?

Hold on, don't put the book down. I don't mean risk assessment like you are thinking. I mean work out the risk posed to your decision making by your personal traits, the environment you find yourself in and your decision-making processes and then manage them. The risk process asks you to understand the context in which you are making a decision, and to analyse how a less-than-optimal decision may be made. Further, it guides you to put in place steps to manage the risks that you have identified and to then get on with making a great decision.

I have already outlined the three key elements of my MCI decision-making model: motivation, clarification and implementation. Later in this book I will introduce you to a process you can follow to manage the risk in your decision making using these three key elements. Before we go to the solution, however, you need to have an appreciation of the risks posed to your decision making.

You are right to be thinking that you manage risk every day. You apply the process. The problem is you are not applying the process well on the bigger strategic decisions. Of course you are not alone, after all, only about 50 percent of our strategic decisions have a successful outcome anyway. Right? Think about the last group of larger, more strategic decisions you made. Where did risk come into the process? If you are like most executives I have worked with, risk either is something discussed informally during the decision-making process or it is something thrown to the risk team at a single point in time to get their views, normally after the decision has already been made. No wonder when the risk team comes back, pointing at all the gaps in your decision-making process you get your back up. Who likes to be told they are wrong? Next you are telling them they are anti-sales, anti-growth, they are a handbrake on business, a group of wet-blanket conservatives whose only pleasure in life is bringing others down.

Consideration of risk is essential to every decision we make because by the nature of the need to decide, we most certainly have uncertainty. You know that. My point is, we have risk management, the single best process in the world today to manage uncertainty and we don't use it to its full potential. I know, I have seen it. I have discussed this with hundreds of risk professionals who see it every day. I have trained and coached risk professionals to learn how to deliver value to their organisations which ultimately win over the most sceptical executive or board director. The best risk professionals win the sceptics back from the dark side of viewing risk as a compliance function. Not through the powers of coercion, not through smoke and mirrors, simply by putting themselves in your shoes, ensuring they understand you and your business, that they have done their homework and that they speak in your language. The language of business or policymakers or entrepreneurs or philanthropists. If they are able to achieve all that, they are able to help executives and board directors of any organisation to make better decisions.

The problem in most organisations, however, is that risk is seen as a process that is added on to how business is done; it has not become part of core decision making. Remember, the three main components you need to consider for every decision are in the MCI model – your motivation to make the decision, clarification of the options available to you and whether you are ready, willing and able to implement your decision. And as you will find out, as I take you through the decision-making process and help you explore the importance of MCI, you will discover there is a world of opportunity to improve decision making that the risk profession and most executives have never realised.

A common trap

Earlier this year, I ran one of my regular free webinars with the topic "What does risk-based decision making really mean?"

It was the second most popular webinar I had run to date. As usual my team sent a recording of the webinar to anyone who registered but was unable to attend. A couple of days later I got an email from one of my clients. He was head of audit and risk at a top-100-listed Australian company. It read as follows:

> I am currently having a debate with a colleague (my boss) regarding the merit of risk-based decision making at a strategic level. The debate centres around strategic-investment decisions and the process used to make those decisions. At a high level my view is that applying a risk-based assessment of the investment decision adds value as it provides another lens which helps to inform the capital-investment decision. However, the alternate view from my colleague is that basing the decision on NPV (net present value) metrics is sufficient as the foundation of the investment decision. I would be interested your comments regarding this scenario.

Rather than replying by email I picked up the phone to make sure I understood the scenario. We discussed what his colleague meant by NPV metrics being sufficient. Indeed, in following the NPV methodology the executive team was considering risk in that they might consider a higher discount rate for a less certain income stream for example. However, as my client pointed out to his colleague, in the absence of a broader based consideration of risk around the entire opportunity, how could he be confident the discount rate reflected the risk?

This is a perfect example of a common trap in decision making. A reliance on a flawed methodology because of a lack of consideration of risk. Informed decision making is much broader than thinking about adjusting a discount rate to compensate for uncertainty. Informed decision making is about understanding the drivers of the uncertainty and how these might be managed to come to a much more well-founded basis for the discount rate. It is also about getting over our seemingly inherent aversion to risk models when it makes sense to use them. Informed decision-making processes, such as risk assessment, could even redefine the entire project because of the strategic imperatives they may uncover – downside or upside. Yes, taking the time to manage the risk in your decision making can drive you to take more risk when you find out how conservative you are actually being, or that your market position is much stronger than previously thought.

How often have you heard about scenario or stress-testing an NPV or other financial model? It is not as bad as it used to be, at least in the finance and oil and gas sectors, where risk models are being used in sophisticated ways after decades of development. However, in so many other industries the test scenarios are simply used to show how cost increases of say 10 or 20 percent would cut into revenue. Often, the scenarios are run without considering the drivers of uncertainty around revenue and costs, or deciding how best they might be managed.

Way too often management teams fall into the trap of doing the analysis, making the decision and then conducting a risk assessment. The risk assessment is often tacked on just to please someone else. Worse still, some teams throw it to the risk team to have a look at after they have made their decision. We all know how that is going to end up more often than not. Because the risk team comes with a different lens, they will come up with issues that need consideration, issues the management team hasn't thought of. Because people don't like being told they are wrong, the risk team's assessment can provoke a defensive reaction. The initial reaction is to start to defend oneself, rather than accept the constructive criticism.

The real problem is that many managers have a bad perception of risk management, to the extent that it is treated like a box-ticking exercise, or an exercise of "getting it through" the risk team. How has this happened? By letting risk be usurped by audit and compliance back office pedants, who make the process complex and who speak a language that is often foreign to management teams. Even a good quality, well-meaning risk manager who also has responsibility for audit and compliance faces this problem. As my client who sent me the email re the NPV method of decision making said, "Every time I walk through the door of a manager's office I can see that all they can see is a big A for auditor on my forehead."

What is needed is people well versed in managing the risk in decision making, taking a seat at the table early in the decision-making process so that all of the decision pitfalls that lead to our 50 percent track record can be identified and avoided as best as possible. In fact, we want executives well versed in managing risk according to the three key MCI components. We want them to assess the risk around their motivation, the risk surrounding their consideration of each option and to assess the risks to the organisation's ability to implement. The implementation is then planned around managing the identified uncertainties, in a way that provides flexibility when other uncertainties arise. If you do this you are going to reach the heady heights of greater than 80 percent of decisions being a success.

Strategic leadership

I said that consideration of risk is essential to every decision. The importance of risk is recognised by most authors of books and papers on decision making. Take Nutt for example. In *Why Decisions Fail,* he has an appendix on estimating risk.[12] However, most of his discussion about risk is around its misuse: the misuse of data, statistics and analysis.

In *Decisive*, Chip and Dan Heath refer to risk in people's decisions throughout the book. They recognise its importance. They say that the 1979 seminal paper on decision making, Daniel Kahneman and Amos Tversky's *Prospect Theory: An Analysis of Decision Under Risk*, is all about understanding our sometimes strange reaction to risk.[13] As the Heaths point out, this paper was published in *The Econometrics Journal*, a respected economic

---

12 Nutt, Paul C (2002). *Why Decisions Fail: Avoiding the Blunders and Traps That Lead to Debacles*, Berrett-Koehler Publishers, San Francisco, CA.

13 Heath, Chip & Dan (2013), *Decisive: How to make better choices in life and work*, Random House, London.

and technical publication and "became the most cited paper ever to appear in the journal". All the more remarkable given Kahneman and Tversky were psychologists and not economists. And there it was, right in front of us 36 years ago. Irrespective, none of the decision-making processes put forward, such as the Heath's WRAP method, deal with risk in the decision-making process explicitly.

What about the tome of all knowledge these days, Wikipedia? Have a search for "decision making" in Wikipedia and then search for "risk". At the time of writing, the combination first pops ups well down in section eight on cognitive and personal biases when referring to, wait for it, prospect theory. I also searched for risk's synonym – uncertainty. This word only gets a mention four lines earlier! It seems we are forgetting the origins of the word "decide".

According to the Merriam-Webster Dictionary, the first known use of the word decide was in the 14th century and it comes from the Latin word "decidere" via Middle English. The meaning of "decidere" was literally to cut off and was derived from combining de- with caedere, to cut. In essence, the word decide is about cutting, or eliminating, choices. By the very fact that we have choices and an unpredictable future, all of our decisions are made within a realm of uncertainty. That means risk. Why then would we not turn to the best proved method ever for dealing with uncertainty – risk management?

Kahneman considers decision researcher and author Paul Slovic as someone "who probably knows more about the peculiarities of human judgement of risk than any other individual".[14] Slovic highlighted the difference in the abilities between some experts and the average lay person to assess risk. A key factor he identified was the ability of the expert to think without emotion of consequences of decisions.

To be sure, other studies show that emotion skews our perceptions. For example, if you are provided with a set of general statistics, say injury and fatality statistics for a particular trade in a particular industry you are likely to consider "that is a reasonable background risk" for the industry. On the other hand, if those statistics are broken down personally for you, so that you are looking at the statistic that directly relates to your potential for injury or even death in working in that industry each year, you are more likely to be surprised at the risk. On a personal level, we are much more risk-averse. We want our own individual chance of death to be as remote as a lightning strike, say one in 10 million, rather than the one in 1,000 that may be the reality. Everybody is different on where these numbers lie, however, the difference between expert and personalised reactions to such statistics is marked.

Throughout *Thinking Fast and Slow*, Kahneman's regular reference to risk and his references to research, his own and that of his friend Amos Tversky, provide all the evidence we need to see how poorly we often assess risk. While Kahneman's processes for identifying and managing the risk-pitfalls that

---

14   http://www.amazon.com/Thinking-Fast-Slow-Daniel-Kahneman

come with fast thinking go a long way to helping us recognise our faults, he also recognises how hard it is to change. He admits his own cognitive biases still exist, saying that although some have tempered with age, none have disappeared despite his years of study of the subject. The problem is, these tendencies are personal and involuntary. It is very difficult to control them. As Kahneman points out, however, when it comes to organisational decision making, there are ways to identify and manage the biases. Organisations have the opportunity to put into place processes to manage decision-making pitfalls.

So, do most organisations put into place good decision-making processes? Ones that manage the fact that the only certainty in decision making is uncertainty? The answer is no. Organisations put into place many governance processes and some provide training in decision making as part of a leadership program. However, many have missed the one big opportunity to take strategic leadership to another level. They have not fully grasped risk-based decision making and applied it through the full continuum of the decision-making process, across the three components of MCI. This continuum starts with what drives us and how we are feeling – motivation, goes through the consideration of options – clarification, and on to a state of relentless execution – implementation, a stage full of sub-routines of decision making that are continually referencing the original decision.

By now I hope that you have a fair idea of where I believe you can take your strategic leadership and the strategic leadership

53

of others in your organisation. The following parts of this book explore each component of the MCI model and the final part explains how you can manage the risk in each component. This will enable you to quickly improve your decision making from the more routine daily decisions required of managers, through to the more demanding decision making required of strategic leaders. As you work through each chapter, remember that it is clearly certain that uncertainty abounds. For the strategic leader, remember uncertainty is not your enemy; it is your best friend. Using the MCI model that I have developed provides the opportunity for you to do the work, to embrace uncertainty and to develop the smarter strategies for strong organisational growth that others will miss or simply avoid.

Part II

It starts with motivation

Chapter 5

Motivation determines mindset

The first and most difficult risk to manage in our decision making is the risk posed by what motivates us.

While writing this book I read of a 19-year-old man's funeral. For all intents and purposes he wasn't much different to me when I was his age. He went to a school I knew and I had played rugby against. He was attending Sydney University, the same university I attended. In the early hours of February 5, 2015 he climbed up a crane on a barge carrying out upgrade work on a local marine facility and he fell into Sydney Harbour. His friend, watching on, never saw him surface. His body was found by police divers a few hours later.

How often have we read these stories? Young men at the prime of their lives taking risks and having their lives ended prematurely, and cruelly. We have all seen the pain and suffering left behind. The difficult truth is that young men take risks, have done for millennia and will continue to do so because it is a physiological response. Scientists know key portions of the brain that control our impulses are less developed in young men. Some young men are also more tempted by these impulses because for each time they get away with something risky, there is a thrill. For some it becomes addictive.

A friend I went to school with was an example of this addictive behaviour that ended in tragedy. John was always a risk taker. He was always in trouble with teachers in primary school and always took the forbidden path on school excursions. As we entered our high-school years, his risk taking became more extreme. I remember one lunchtime looking up from the school quadrangle to see him hanging by his fingertips from a brick balcony that ran outside our classrooms. He was three storeys up with concrete below. I remember thinking how extra crazy it was given the way the bricks were slightly curved for an aesthetic look, and making them more difficult to hang on to.

After school John became a pilot, got into drugs and ended up in jail for a period. Unfortunately his time in jail did not change his penchant for risk taking. His final act of risk taking occurred on May 21, 1989. In the early hours of the morning he and a friend stole a Beechraft Baron from Bankstown airport, in Sydney. The Baron is a twin-engined light plane that seats a maximum of five passengers. According to the aviation safety investigation report, the Baron took off without any contact with air traffic control. Witnesses said the plane was being flown erratically as it was tracked by radar to Bringelly about 25 kilometres west where it crashed through trees, coming to rest on fire in a small dam. John and his friend were both killed.

When I heard about the crash I was living in Toronto, Canada and was being visited by an old high-school buddy of mine. He and I received the news via a letter from home. While shocked, we both commented on how it had seemed inevitable. You hear the expression "He had a death wish". Well that might have been said about John. I think it was more that he simply needed to keep having thrills. He was addicted to risk taking.

What motivates you leads you

What about Andrew McAuley, an Australian adventurer who went missing, presumed dead, in 2007 on his second attempt to make a solo kayak cross the Tasman Sea from Australia to New Zealand. What motivated McAuley? His first attempt at the 2,000-kilometre crossing was aborted after only two days due to, according to his blog post at the time, his inability to keep warm inside the specially built cockpit. At the time of his death he was married and had a small child. As a father of three myself, I thought him crazy and irresponsible. When I dug deeper into his background, I began to change my mind.

McAuley was awarded Adventurer of the Year in 2005 by the Australian Geographic Society and in 2007 its Lifetime of Achievement Award, posthumously. His history as an adventurer included mountain climbing. He was better known though for his kayaking feats. He crossed Bass Straight from Australia's mainland to Tasmania (220 kilometres), the Gulf of Carpentaria (530 kilometres) and made an expedition of more than 800 kilometres into Antarctica.[15] As you can see, he was more than a little experienced and was taking on increasingly greater challenges. Each time he learnt from the last expedition and more went into his planning, none more so than his planning for crossing the Tasman. In a blog posted by his support crew shortly before McAuley went missing they gave us a good feeling of the level of planning. Despite all of the things that went wrong, he very nearly made it.

> For your interest, the tally of equipment failure thus far …
> tracking beacon (carked it after first capsize 3 weeks ago);
> secondary sat phone (suffered same fate in same capsize);
> watch (no longer knows what time it is, so he's figuring if it's
> dark, it must be time to transmit his report!); broken pivot arm
> on Casper (apparently not affecting his performance); cracked
> lens on bullet camera (we'll have to look at stripey footage!).
> That's all we know of … we'll get the whole story in a couple
> of days!!

Crazy? Irresponsible? I think not. Driven? More motivated than almost any of us? Yes.

---

15 Andrew McAuley. (2015, October 14). In *Wikipedia, the Free Encyclopedia*. Retrieved 01:11, October 22, 2015, from https://en.wikipedia.org/w/index. php?title=Andrew_McAuley&oldid=685631396

So what drives people like McAuley? This blog from his website posted by his support crew shortly after he was declared missing, presumed dead, provides us with some insight.

> *Man cannot discover new oceans unless he has the courage to lose sight of the shore.*
>
> – Andre Gide

Feb 18, 2007: At 7.15pm NZ time on Friday 9th February, the New Zealand coastguard received an almost indecipherable transmission on channel 16 from a vessel identifying itself as 'Kayak 1' in the Fiordland. Andrew was within sight of land.

When no further communication was received, ships in the area were diverted to investigate. A full-scale aerial search ensued, and Andrew's kayak was located, capsized, late the following evening approximately 30 nautical miles off the coast of New Zealand. Andrew was not found, yet his spirit will live on forever. In my mind, he achieved his goal.

Ant, you live for adventure, and you've just had the most incredible adventure this time. We were with you all the way! You have lived life to the fullest, and you'll live on in our hearts forever!

Andrew's family and support team wish to express our utmost appreciation and thanks to all those involved in the search – the New Zealand Rescue Coordination Centre, the Te Anau police, the Australian government and all the wonderful New Zealand local people who have extended their hearts and offers of help in this most difficult time. We are indebted to you all.

We are extremely proud of Andrew and will always remain so. His incredible achievements in adventuring are without parallel. Whilst being driven by the challenge of making the impossible possible, much of Andrew's motivation was also based on inspiring others to get up and have a go at exploring their own limits. He was and will continue to be an inspiration to others in their own personal endeavours.

Ant, we love you and will miss you more than words can express.

So McAuley found his strength, his inner drive from wanting to "make the impossible possible"and from "inspiring others to get up and have a go at exploring their limits". McAuley had found his purpose in life and it was a strong, higher-order one. It drove him very hard just like it has driven explorers, leaders and great philanthropists throughout history.

Motivation determines mindset and our motivation can be very strong. Sometimes it can defeat us. Was this the case for Andrew McAuley?

What motivates you can also defeat you – McAuley

As I researched Andrew McAuley's story I found one piece of information that made me question his motivation to attempt the crossing of the Tasman Sea at that particular time. I was listening to Richard Fidler interview two other adventurers, Justin Jones and James Castrission, on ABC radio. This duo were also kayak adventurers and knew of McAuley's success and hence his capabilities. During the interview, they explained that they had visited McAuley to talk about their ambition to be the first to cross the Tasman by kayak.

Picture McAuley as accomplished explorer and the most experienced and celebrated ocean kayaker in Australia. Along come Castrission and Jones asking McAuley for his advice to help them be the first to cross the Tasman by kayak. In the 2014 interview, Castrission explained that he and Jones gave McAuley their risk-management document, their blueprint for crossing the Tasman.[16] He went on to say, "We idolised Andrew at that stage. Unfortunately, it was just a hard thing to get a phone call a couple of weeks later from one of our team saying that Andrew is actually putting together an expedition to cross the Tasman." Fidler then asked, "So then it became a race for you guys?" and the conversation flowed as below:

Jones: We met up with Andrew again and had a chat to him about what was actually going on and you could see a man that was torn. He was confused, he told us that he hadn't slept for three nights when he found out about our plans. It

16 Fidler, Richard (Presenter) and James Castrission and Justin Jones (Guests). (2014, August 27). James Castrission and Justin Jones kayaked the Tasman Sea [Radio broadcast]. Sydney, Australia: ABC. See, http://www.abc.net.au/local/stories/2014/08/27/4075444.htm

was something that he had always planned and dreamt of doing himself and to see two other guys going out there and doing it he felt the urge to get out there and give the Tasman a go.

Fidler: So this was a dream he'd always had and he just couldn't bear the thought of someone doing it ahead of him?

Jones: I think we kind of pushed him out the door a little bit in that regards, I mean he probably thought, "In x amount of years I'm going to attempt a crossing, at this stage once I've done this amount of preparation" but then I suppose we popped up and said, "These are our plans, this is our blueprint, this is how we're going to do it" and he was like, "Geez, I've got to get a wriggle-on. I've got to start moving on this project if I want to be the first to cross it."

From this evidence it seems to me that what McAuley needed was a decision-making process that would allow him to assess the risk in his decision making. A process that would allow him to properly articulate and understand his true motivation.

What can be inferred is that McAuley's overriding desire was to be the first. This is one time that it seems he let desire trump purpose. If his purpose was "the challenge of making the impossible possible", and "inspiring others to get up and have a go at exploring their own limits", shouldn't McAuley have been pleased for Castrission and Jones, and shouldn't he have been supportive?

While no one but McAuley may ever know, the scenario detailed here begs the question: did the visit by Castrission and Jones prompt McAuley to rush through the detailed planning and kayak design work for his attempt because he couldn't bear the thought of not being the first to make the Tasman crossing?

What motivates you can also defeat you – NASA

In an earlier chapter, I mentioned the successful moon landing in 1969, which was the pinnacle of Project Apollo. For those old enough, we can remember exactly where we were when we watched the televised landing.

The successful moon landing marked the entire Project Apollo, a success even though it took longer and cost more than planned and it cost the lives of three men. NASA itself provides a great research resource via their history website where the underlying reasons for the success of the Apollo program are well articulated.[17] I have drawn from the website to summarise the program:

Desire: Project Apollo was created out of a strong desire. In 1961, when the US and the Soviet Union were in the middle of the Cold War, the Soviets had the first win with their space program by launching Yuri Gagarin as the first man into space. So, when President Kennedy announced the US plan to land a man on the moon before the end of the decade, the desire was stronger than ever to succeed.

---

17 Launius, Roger D. (1994). *Apollo: A retrospective analysis*. NASA. Washington, D.C. From: See: http://history.nasa.gov/Apollomon/Apollo.html

Capacity: NASA obviously had capabilities. In addition, appropriate levels of funding were available because of the strong US economy and, bolstered with an influx of migrants post the Second World War, NASA had access to a highly skilled workforce.

Budget and timetable: Officials were able to gain approval for a budget of US$35 billion (in 1970) which gave them a 75 percent margin for error over their initial budget. They had also estimated they could deliver by 1967, however, they were able to extract a two-year contingency margin. It is interesting to note that the final cost, estimated in 1970, was US$24 billion, or about US$90 billion in today's dollars.

Resources: "By 1966 the agency's civil service rolls had grown to 36,000 people from the 10,000 employed at NASA in 1960. Outside researchers and technicians meant contractor employees working on the program increased by a factor of 10, from 36,500 in 1960 to 376,700 in 1965. Private industry, research institutions and universities, therefore, provided the majority of personnel working on Apollo.

Support: The US people were fully behind the project and so were the politicians.

Program management: The NASA administration understood the enormity of their challenge and consequently "an omnipotent program office with centralized authority over design, engineering, procurement, testing, construction, manufacturing, spare parts, logistics, training, and operations" was created. NASA went on to say, "It may turn out that [the space program's] most valuable spin-off of all will be human rather than technological: better knowledge of how to plan, coordinate, and monitor the multitudinous and varied activities of the organizations required to accomplish great social undertakings."

Wind forward two decades and NASA is in full swing with its space shuttle program. The date is January 28, 1986. This is another day in history when, if you were old enough, you can remember exactly where you were.

For Roger Boisjoly, it was a day where he lived a nightmare. In the book *Inviting Disaster*[18] under the chapter "Rush to Judgment – When flagship projects run out of time," author James Chiles tells Boisjoly's story.

Boisjoly was an engineer at Morton Thiokol, the firm responsible for the design of the space shuttle solid rocket boosters that sent US space shuttles into orbit. Their design included the O-ring that failed on the Challenger shuttle. In simple terms, Challenger was launched via two solid rocket boosters that would separate from the external fuel tank that fed fuel to the space shuttle's engines. The external tank would also jettison once it was expended leaving the shuttle to fly the last part of the journey into orbit utilising its own power sources. Solid rocket fuel is advantageous because you get more power-to-weight ratio than with liquid fuel. And it is less complicated,

18 Chiles, James R (2001). *Inviting disaster: lessons from the edge of technology: an inside look at catastrophes and why they happen*, Harper Collins, N.Y.

in that liquid fuel needs refrigeration and pressurisation, whereas the solid rocket fuel did not.

The solid rocket boosters contained several joints sealed by rubber O-rings, which were designed to contain the hot, burning gases as they shot through the booster to be released at the booster's base, thus creating the propulsion. If an O-ring failed, hot burning gases at high pressure would flow out of the seal and, depending on where the failure was and how big it was, the flames could impinge on the external fuel tank.

I'll let Chiles take over from here:

> Boisjoly had done all a loyal engineer could do to persuade his company, Morton Thiokol, to persuade NASA not to launch the shuttle during the bitter cold temperatures predicted for the next day at Kennedy Space Center.
>
> At the start of the 8:45 P.M. EST teleconference between offices in Utah, Florida, and Alabama, things looked good for Boisjoly and several others at Thiokol who wanted NASA to hold off on the launch until warmer weather. Solid rocket manager Allan J. McDonald warned NASA managers that as company representative he would not sign the launch recommendation. He advised NASA not to proceed until the weather warmed enough to bring the boosters up to 53°F. Otherwise the rubber "O-ring" seals connecting the booster segments might leak, let gas burn through the steel casing, and cause a catastrophic failure.

NASA representatives replied over the telecon link that the leaking-seal problem was a known quantity and under control, and they added that there was no conclusive link between cold O-rings and leaks, anyway. After all, one of the worst gas leaks had happened when a booster was very warm. NASA engineers felt Thiokol's proposed lower limit of 53°F was not supported by any evidence and was inconsistent with the lower temperatures that Thiokol had already accepted during previous wintertime launch attempts. Booster manager Larry Mulloy wrapped up this point of view by demanding over the telecon line, "My God, Thiokol, when do you want us to launch—next April?"

After a thirty-minute break, Thiokol's engineer managers reported back that they would withdraw their objections. Since McDonald wouldn't put his name on the recommendation, booster-program vice president Joe Kilminster signed a form instead and faxed it to NASA. Boisjoly opened his journal that night and jotted down his feelings of anger and worry. At work the next morning, Boisjoly stopped by his boss's office to say that he hoped for a safe flight but also wished the seal on a joint would leak just enough to prove beyond all doubt that a serious problem existed. After Boisjoly left and was walking down the hall, ignition-systems manager Bob Ebeling asked him to step inside a conference room and watch the launch on the big TV. Boisjoly said no, but Ebeling insisted. Boisjoly worked his way to an open spot in the front of the room, sitting on the floor with his back against Ebeling's legs. Sixty seconds into the flight, Ebeling said a prayer of thanks for a safe flight.

The Challenger broke up thirteen seconds later, painting puffy white streamers across the sky and throwing the room at the Wasatch Division headquarters into a dazed disbelief.

Boisjoly spent the rest of the day in his office, not even able to speak when people stopped by to ask how he was doing. He was not surprised the next day when a fellow employee told him that a videotape during launch showed a flame leak through a joint in the booster case, just before the disaster.

Although the space shuttle program was a magnificent achievement that advanced our knowledge of flight, space and human endurance, it cost the lives of 14 astronauts in two separate events. What was their mindset for the launch of the Challenger? Billions of dollars were spent, which added pressure from politicians and bureaucrats; the high public profile built expectations, and the media was feeding the public hunger for national success. And there was also self-induced pressure: the pressure to succeed in this difficult challenge with all eyes watching. All of these pressures were there all of the time at NASA. The organisation was used to it and its people had a can-do attitude. Was anything different leading up to the launch of Challenger that meant the pressure had increased?

The Rogers Presidential Commission report into the Challenger accident found that there was something different.[19]

---

19 Presidential Commission on Space Shuttle Challenger & Rogers, W. P. (1986). *Report of the Presidential Commission on the Space Shuttle Challenger Accident.* p.170.

The commission reflected on the pressures on management that came as NASA fell further and further behind their publicly declared launch rates. According to the commission, the proposed flight rate was originally set at an ambitious one per week, then reduced to a planned 24 per year by 1990. In 1985, nine missions were launched and by early 1986, in the lead up to the ill-fated Challenger launch, the 15 flights scheduled for the year were not looking likely. NASA had underestimated the resources it would take to fulfil such a demand.

With the increased pressure, the whole context for the launch decision had changed. During the commission hearing, Morton Thiokol's vice president engineering, Bob Lund, testified that in hindsight the decision-making process for their launch recommendation had been reversed for the Challenger launch. Instead of being in a situation where they had to prove to NASA that it was safe to launch, they instead had to prove it that it was not safe. And as Lund put it, "We couldn't prove absolutely that the motor wouldn't work."[20]

With a must-launch mindset, the only thing left to the decision makers regarding the Challenger launch was to consider the risk in their decision-making process. Unfortunately they, like so many other management teams, did not consider the risk in their decision-making process and the tragedy unfolded. The presidential commission found "that there was a serious

---

20 Presidential Commission on Space Shuttle Challenger & Rogers, W. P. (1986). *Report of the Presidential Commission on the Space Shuttle Challenger Accident.* p. 95.

flaw in the decision-making process leading up to the launch", with a lack of an emphasis on safety. Further, the commission found that because there was no requirement for "waivers of launch constraints" (which is essentially what happened with Morton-Thiokol going against its own requirements for the launch temperature for the O-ring) to be communicated higher up the decision-making chain to more senior decision makers. Testifying under oath, the Kennedy Space Centre director, the launch director and the associate administrator for space flight, all stated that they were not aware of any of the objections of the Morton-Thiokol team.

With the benefit of Harry Hindsight, it is obvious the key decision makers at the time did not sit and think about the risk posed to people's decision making that this level of pressure was creating. If they had, there may have been a different result. In the case of Challenger, the risk the O-ring posed had been identified. However, the pressure felt by decision makers from external stakeholder expectations was enough to cloud decision making. The pressure they felt created a must-launch mindset which led to disaster.

Mindset can be a magnificent attribute to attain levels of success not imaginable by many. However, a growth mindset without consideration of the risk it poses is dangerous. On the other hand, a fixed mindset without an understanding of the risk it poses is just as bad as it may freeze you from taking much-needed action or to grasp opportunities.

Chapter 6

Mindset creates blockers

Have you thought much about the question: What is your purpose in life? I mean really thought about it? I don't blame you if you haven't as it is a big question with the potential for a whole lot of angst. For many, religion has found its place in their hearts, for others it is scientific endeavours and for others like Andrew McAuley, it is showing that the boundary that defines impossibility can be pushed further and further back.

Purpose, for many of us, is something that becomes more relevant the longer we travel along life's journey. It is in the back of our minds, sitting there quietly waiting to rise up, or gnawing at us, impatiently. As children we are very focused on ourselves. As teenagers we learn many altruistic values and then as adolescents many of our desires take control. Desires for freedom, for the excitement of new things in new places, desires to express ourselves sexually. Before long comes the desire to work out what "to do" in life. In working out what "to do" in life, a whole lot of other challenges present themselves. Perhaps we have left the nest and need to fend for ourselves, perhaps where we live is not a very prosperous part of the world and the need for the basics in life take over.

When you consider the journey of life, you can see that our motivation changes. Indeed, it can change quite dramatically as circumstances change. Let's take a little anthropological view of life for a moment. How has our basic, human survival instinct become our key motivator? Here's a hint: hot versus cold.

In warmer climates, as humans evolved we were blessed with, shall we say, "the easy life" when it comes to the basics of nourishment. We could pick berries, and hunt a range of animals and fish to our heart's content. In colder climates, we had to start working on ways to survive the harsh winters, develop ways to build appropriate shelters and stockpile food. Because of the environment we found ourselves in, we were motivated in different ways and, consequently, there was a stronger development of food-and-shelter storing techniques in colder climates.

Purpose is at one end of the spectrum of things that drive our motivation. Survival is at the other end. What is in between?

Do you understand what drives your motivation?

When I think about what motivates us I think of three things. Survival, desire and purpose. For me they are a simple hierarchy.

Survival, the base instinct to survive is the strongest driving force of all. Once we are safe, with food and shelter, we are able to move onto things we may desire such as the modern-day desires of a better restaurant experience or a fancier home. Fortunately, for many of us, there is a higher driver; and that is purpose.

Where does purpose come from? In his book *Genome*, Matt Ridley opines several times that who we are seems to be about half nature, half nurture.[21] He describes behavioural tendencies linked to specific genes, others that have no genetic links and some which are a mixture.

Ridley also concludes that specific genes have mutated in response to our behaviour. He provides an example of all the herding tribes among our ancestors, who developed a gene mutation enabling them to digest lactose. Because they were the first to develop the ability to digest lactose, his conclusion is that our herding behaviour drove the gene mutation.

We all know that people are able to change. Social programs, drug and alcohol-rehabilitation programs and even jails can all change people for the better, although jails have the reputation for doing the opposite to many inmates. One of the most famous examples in Australia of changing for the better is the story of two drug smugglers – Andrew Chan and Myuran Sukumaran. These men were convicted and sentenced to death for being the ring leaders of a drug-trafficking group dubbed the Bali Nine.

---

21 Ridley, M. (1999), *Genome, The Autobiography of a Species in 23 Chapters*, The Fourth Estate, London.

After 10 years in an Indonesian jail they had rehabilitated. They had developed a reputation in Kerobokan prison as fine men who were helping to change others. Sukumaran taught English, computer studies, graphic design and philosophy classes to inmates and was instrumental in creating a computer and art room. He was also appointed the head of a group of more than 20 prisoners, including some facing execution. Chan became a Christian while in prison, was a mentor to many of the inmates, led the English-language church service and started a certificate course at Harvest Bible College. While the cynics among us may say that they were only doing so to save their own lives, they sustained their reformed behaviour for years. A hard act to keep up if you were not wholeheartedly serious about it. The greatest irony came in their executions, 10 years after their crimes, and only after they had been rehabilitated into good men who were helping others within Kerobokan.

Thinking of Chan and Sukumaran, one has to wonder what drove them to commit crimes with such a high risk attached. The death penalty in Indonesia for drug trafficking was well publicised in Australia and at every entry point into Indonesia. There had been high-profile Australians executed for drug offences in the region in the not too far distant past.

It seems they were caught within the desire level of motivation. The incentives they saw likely included the financial benefits of crime, the personal triumph they might feel for pulling off the crime, and maybe even how big they would feel being thought of as drug barons among their associates back in Australia. These sort of desires were a stronger pull than the values that they had had instilled in them. The values that help to determine our purpose.

When you look at business CEOs, do you see their motivation as survival, desire or purpose? Do you see the current environment being the key driver causing them to look to survive, or do you see incentives for organisational and personal success driving their desires? Perhaps you see a value system driving them to define a higher purpose for the organisation? You have probably seen CEOs and other senior people with all of these motivators. Some successful, and some not so successful, no matter which motivational state they are working in. Some successful in one state and not in another. Why is that?

In her book *Mindset*, Carol S. Dweck relates the story of Lee Iacocca who worked at Ford, was fired, became CEO of Chrysler at the time it was on the brink of financial failure, turned it around and then broke it again before he was "eased out" by the board.[22] In her book, Dweck boils things down to two mindsets that people have, fixed and growth. The fixed mindset creates a pattern of proving oneself as right, whereas a growth mindset recognises imperfection and has a willingness to learn and hence grow.

Iacocca was a classic example of the fixed mindset, says Dweck. At Ford he had learnt about the good life while also learning how to run a car company. He was close to the top

---

22 Dweck, Dr Carol S (2012). *Mindset: How you can fulfil your potential*. Little, Brown Book Group, London, pp 114-117.

when he was fired. The state Chrysler was in was perfect for Iacocca's fixed and very determined mindset. He was relentless in his pursuit to prove those at Ford wrong for letting him go. He turned the organisation around and profits flowed. Then desire took over Iacocca.

Referencing Iacocca's autobiography, Dweck paints the picture of a man who desired to be seen as the king and to live a life of royalty.[23] Once he had saved Chrysler and money flowed, his self interest inflated. He became caught in the desire state. He desired the money, the royal court and above all, to be seen as the king of the court. Dweck explains how Iacocca would work to ensure no one else could be seen as the saviour of Chrysler. He would undermine his direct reports and those that took over after he was moved out. He even was a key player in a failed takeover bid in an attempt to regain control of Chrysler and his "rightful" place at the top. According to Dweck, this behaviour cemented for those in doubt that Iacocca only had his own wellbeing in mind whenever he acted.

Like so many before him, Iacocca was caught in the desire state of motivation. He was unable to move to the purpose stage, which would have let him rise above the question of who was king and let his team continue to build on the great platform he had erected.

By now you would have thought about what motivates you in various situations. When it comes to your work life, if you are

---

23 Ibid, p. 114.

not the owner or CEO and you are not setting the vision of the organisation, you are probably working in the desire space, albeit the desire space to help make a difference towards the higher purpose set by the CEO. All the research into organisational culture and wellbeing over the past decade has pointed to the importance of purpose to ensure that employees are engaged and performing. However, if you have not been part of setting the organisation's purpose, are you not simply motivated by desire to fulfil the purpose as it has been set? Maybe so, however, I believe the higher order purpose is at play here. If you were aiming to fulfil purpose so as to be promoted or earn more money, then you are actually stuck in the desire phase and at risk of falling into the trap that Iacocca fell into.

The most important thing is to be fully aware of what it is that's motivating you when you make a decision. That is not always easy to see.

Enough blocks to build a building

The question of what goes on inside our head has many fields of study: from psychiatry and general psychology to economics and sales and marketing. I think of the scientists and researchers in these fields in the same way as I think about the scientists and researchers of the great frontiers of space and the depths of our oceans. While the last 50 years has grown our knowledge base about the brain exponentially, we really only understand a small portion of the whole picture. In space-exploration terms, when it comes to the brain we probably have a good understanding of our solar system. I suggest that those that are at the forefront of their field would even argue we understand the galaxy we live in. However, given the universe is made up of perhaps hundreds of billions of galaxies like our Milky Way, even understanding the galaxy is only a very small portion.

Using a different analogy, I think that in 100 years' time, scientists will look back at our era and see a version of what we see when we look back a century, at the world before penicillin or anaesthetics. The scientists of 2100 will wonder how hard it must have been to have millions of people suffering from so many incurable psychiatric illnesses. They will be looking back at us, taking pity that we weren't able to diagnose mental illnesses in potential thieves, murderers, mass murderers and megalomaniacs and treat them well before they could do any harm.

When it comes to decision making, scientists and researchers have been significant in driving understanding of the processes involved. In the 1970s, it was the work of psychologists Daniel Kahneman and Amos Tversky that seems to have started the flood gates opening. While Tversky passed away in 1996, Kahneman lived on and continued their great work.

In his books, Kahneman often speaks about the hours he spent with Tversky pondering one thing or another about judgement and decision making. He said they were fascinated by their experiments that involved observing others make poor judgements due to their biases. He also observed his own vulnerability to bias. It is no wonder that his most recent work,

Thinking Fast and Slow, has a fundamental premise which any one of us can use to improve our decision making. His tip is to find ways to recognise when you are thinking fast, when in fact it is a time to think slow.

Understanding the modes of fast thinking is key to also understanding the risk fast thinking poses. Let's take a look at the key heuristics, or imperfect gut instincts, that influence us: anchoring, availability, representative, affect and confirmation.

Anchoring. Anchoring is a psychological phenomenon where we are strongly influenced by the first thing we hear about a decision. That is why when you are negotiating the price of something, if you are selling you should start high with an offer and if you are buying you should start low. In a decision context, if the boss asks the proponent of the business case what the bottom-line would be if the plan does not work so well, they will be "anchored" to that number and less able to shift toward a different reality as new information is presented. So, assuming you are presented with the most likely business case, what is the risk in asking each of the following people for an assessment of the upside and downside of the plan?:

1. The proponent of the business case.
2. The analyst who prepared the business case.
3. An independent peer reviewer.

The answer for the proponent of the business case should be clear. They will be driven by their desire to see the project get up and be biased toward the upside. If there is any strong bias in the analyst's views, it will be the desire to be seen as a good analyst. They might tend toward a limited range from downside to upside to show how strong their prediction is. When it comes to the peer reviewer, their answer is "potentially lots of risk". The peer reviewer may have been overlooked for the project or the job of analysing and may start with a negative view. They could be overly friendly with the proponent. They could be a strong potential beneficiary if the project gets up or if it is rejected. These are all potential drivers of motivation that could present a risk. Then you also have the potential risk that the peer review may come up with an answer which would delay the project. And, sometimes, the biggest risk in decision making is not making a decision at all.

Availability. Availability refers to our tendency to judge likelihood based on our own experience. For example, if you weren't friends with any real estate agents and you had only dealt with a few of them and each one of them appeared to lie to you, you might consider the likelihood of finding an honest real estate agent as very low. Whereas if you work in an industry where you are dealing with real estate agents every day, you will form an opinion based on a much larger sample base.

In a business-decision context, senior people who are across news in their industry will be well aware of the events that make the bigger headlines. If they don't have a complete understanding, or aren't as familiar with the specific issue, then the news will often make them more risk averse. Take the growth of the role of social media in business over the past 10 years.

How many organisations were slow to take it up because senior management people were wary of it? They didn't understand it and they thought it frivolous, or childish? Every time an example of social media going wrong for an organisation hit the headlines, the leery would pounce on it as evidence that steering clear of social media was a wise choice.

For sure, while some organisations had problems on the social-media learning curve, there were plenty that were successfully embracing it. Of course, the media was drawn to the scandals and disaster stories. They also reported some tremendous success stories. I believe that one of the greatest risks posed to good decision making over the past decade concerned a fear of being the subject of social-media-disaster reporting. A better consideration of risk in the decision-making process of many organisations would have resulted in opportunities for growth to be identified and taken.

Representative. The representative heuristic is a bit like the old saying "same-same". That is, I have seen this before and so it will be again. In a business context, just because the product launched successfully last time and this one looks similar, it's not safe to assume that it will be. An example of how the representative heuristic can cause a downfall may be that of the failure of the P76 car to meet the automakers' expectations. The P76 motor vehicle was launched in Australia in 1973 by Leyland Australia, a subsidiary of British Leyland. While I have no evidence that decision makers fell into the trap of "how can we fail", I do remember the massive advertising campaign at the time. It was a big spend which would indicate strong confidence in the likelihood of product success.

Although Leyland had obviously launched many cars before, they had not launched a vehicle of the size of the P76 before. It was big with a powerful V8 engine. It was launched following the success of other large cars in the Australian market, including popular models such as the Holden Kingswood and the Ford Falcon.

The P76 did have a lot going for it and so perhaps there was no representative bias in the decision-making process. However, despite winning *Wheels* magazine "Car of the Year" in the year of its launch, the P76 failed to sell well enough to maintain production.

What went wrong? The answer is plenty. There were supply issues, quality problems and a timing issue, with a drop in demand for large gas guzzlers as an oil crisis hit. Perhaps because of past successes, not enough was done by Leyland to think through what it would take to make sure the P76 would be as successful as its earlier models. Certainly, not enough attention was paid to the areas of quality and supply.

Affect. The affect heuristic relates to how we are influenced by what and who we like. For example, assuming you like and trust your mother, you will tend to be more influenced by her on a decision than by someone who you perceive has a similar level of expertise as your mother.

When we are making business decisions we are influenced by our like or dislike for people involved in the decision-influencing process. Of course, with good decision-making structures in place we can temper this, however, by only listening to who we like, we can set ourselves up for a so-called "Bay of Pigs". The Bay of Pigs is usually attributed to the phenomenon referred to as group think, where too many people, thinking alike, wanting the same thing, don't ask enough critical questions, and find out, after the fact, that an idea was not so good after all. I believe you can equally put the Bay of Pigs debacle down to the affect heuristic.

The Bay of Pigs was the 1961 failed US invasion of Cuba. The CIA had trained and armed the Cuban rebels whose aim was to overthrow the Cuban president, Fidel Castro. The US administration assumed that the Cuban people would welcome them, but when they didn't, the attack failed.

At the time President John Kennedy was the golden boy of the US. He was charismatic and he was a winner. You can well imagine his team being in awe of him, believing in his abilities and feeling that he could do no wrong.

The affect heuristic also concerns things you like or dislike. Take the insurance industry. You will often hear people talk about it as a relationship industry. Let's face it, insurance is a grudge purchase and it is difficult for buyers to distinguish between one insurer's product and another's until a claim is made. When you are an insurer selling to clients through insurance brokers, you want insurance brokers on your side so that your product gets a fair hearing by the client.

When I worked in the insurance industry in the 1990s it was

still a male-dominated profession, although it was changing. When someone was deciding which relationship-building exercise to spend their money on, guess which ones came up trumps most often? Sport and boozy lunches or dinners.

On one occasion, when I was in a position to offer something a bit different to our insurance broker clientele, I learnt a valuable lesson. Through a connection, I was able to access 10 tickets at a ridiculously low price to a major speaking event which included retired Major-General Norman Schwarzkopf who led the coalition forces during the first Iraq war in the early 1990s. Another speaker was the Australian stockbroker Rene Rivkin, author of *The Rivkin Report* for budding investors. Our broker clients came away very impressed. This was something different: intellectually stimulating and personally and professionally rewarding. The industry was shifting and becoming more professional and this was an early indication of how organisations could be in front of the curve, avoid the affect heuristic and think more creatively about what is best for the business. My company also took guests to the ballet and opera. They were smart when it came to relationship marketing, appreciating that everyone has different tastes.

Confirmation. Last but not least, the confirmation heuristic, which is about how we tend to hear information that confirms our thinking, and ignore that which doesn't. Take the example of when you have said to your partner, "I think we should go to such and such restaurant," and she says, "Are you sure? I think we should go to so and so." Your partner then suggests that you check them out on a restaurant review site. You are likely to fall for the confirmation heuristic when you get on the site. If the restaurant you wanted to go to has the highest rating, that is all the confirmation you needed. If it is lower than the one that your partner suggested, you will start looking at the comments. You will look for positive comments about the restaurant you chose and negative comments about the restaurant your partner suggested. If you let your partner get online, you might see a very different picture presented.

In business, many team leaders feel the need to be right at least most of the time. These leaders will be more susceptible to the confirmation heuristic. The classic example is the leader who isn't strong numerically, which in my experience is often. If they don't like what the data is saying, what do they say? "Lies, lies, damned lies and statistics." They will opt for the easily disproven myth that anyone can get statistics to tell you whatever answer you want. While this is true for the less numerate, for those who aren't scared of numbers, statistics are your friend.

What have we learnt from the field of psychology, and particularly from the development of these concepts around heuristics? Heuristics present a risk to your decision making, a risk you will need a process for managing. A process for deciding when a heuristic is the best choice of decision-making method and when it is not.

Part III

Clarify your options

Chapter 7

Clarity does not come easily

Our motivation, and the mindset it creates, can be wonderful. However, sometimes they create barriers that we cannot see past, that make us blind to critical information, when we make decisions. Similarly, we can be blind to key information if we have not sought to clarify what is in front of us. Stop looking in the mirror, you will only see the same answer. If you truly understand your motivations and your blockers you can open yourself up to more possibilities, options you might never have considered. Options that will ensure your survival, deliver your desires or help you fulfil your purpose.

Hard-smart work

We all have an image from cartoons of the light bulb going on inside our heads. Remember, it is a cartoon! Much more often than not, clarity does not come by chance. Clarity comes from hard-smart work. What is hard-smart work? It's the work that your competitors won't or can't do and that gives you the competitive edge. The work that only you and your team are able to do because you have thought about it smarter, and worked on understanding it harder than anyone else.

The story of the Linotype machine is a perfect example. In the late 19th century, despite being introduced around 200 years earlier, newspapers were only a few pages long. This was mainly because of the cost of printing as the plates for print runs were set by hand, letter by letter. There were fast printing presses which produced thousands and thousands of copies quickly, but to capture the daily news and get it to the masses, the laborious step of compositing the text limited production to a small number of pages.

The race had been on for decades to find ways of automating the process in order to cut costs and increase production. American novelist Mark Twain was one who could see the upside in creating a solution and he invested a huge amount of his wealth into the Paige Compositor. This investment is one commonly attributed with causing his bankruptcy. Why did the Paige Compositor fail? Because it was not nearly as good as the Linotype Machine invented by Ottmar Mergenthaler.[24]

The Linotype machine was the brainchild of the combination of a court reporter James Ogilvie Clephane, "mechanic" Charles

---

24 Lienhard, John (2000). *The Paige Compositor: Engines of Our Ingenuity*, Houston University, Houston.

T. Moore[25] and trained watchmaker Mergenthaler. What a combination. Clephane, while driven to report faster, was also a venture capitalist[26] so money was available. Together, with Moore's smarts for mechanics and Mergenthaler's smarts in watchmaking, they invented one of the most amazing machines ever built. In action, it's like a very large watch moving smoothly and rapidly. I was a bit surprised to learn that the Linotype machine only replaced a half a dozen people doing the compositing. I would have thought it would have been 20 or 30. Goes to show how fast the typesetters of the 1800s actually were.

The Linotype machine of the 19th century combined a keyboard with a magazine of letters that were slotted into a line of type. Each letter was injection moulded with molten metal, eventually forming a line of type on the print plate. In his episode on the Paige Compositor for his "Engines of Ingenuity" radio program at the University of Houston, John Leinhard spoke of the difference in the approaches of the inventor of the Paige Compositor and that of the creators of the Linotype.[27] According to Leinhard, Paige built his device based on a study of human-hand movement, while Mergenthaler based his on what he knew a machine could do. The Paige Compositor had

25 Rollins, Lawrence E. (1937). "Charles T. Moore – Arrogant Mechanic." *The West Virginia Review*. vol. 14, no. 10, p. 338. Via: http://www.circuitousroot.com/ artifice/letters/press/noncastcomp/moore/

26 Brody, J. E. (2007, December 11). "Mental reserves keep brain agile," *The New York Times*. Retrieved from: http://query.nytimes.com/gst/abstract.html?res=980 6E1DE1638E333A25752C0A9649D946196D6CF

27 Lienhard, op cit.

18,000 parts with much more chance of breakdowns and was more expensive than the Linotype Machine.

As you consider your next investment, consider what Twain said about his experience with the Paige Compositor. The lesson: "Not to invest when you can't afford to and not to invest when you can".[28]

The winners, Clephane, Moore and Mergenthaler worked together over almost two decades to produce the Linotype machine. These determined hard-smart workers went from idea, to patent to prototype, again and again until they found the gold. While there is always an element of luck when it comes to beating scores of other inventors working over decades, one can't help but reflect on their determination and their intelligence. Their invention was still producing the *New York Times* in 1978, almost a century later.[29] It led to an explosion in literacy as reading material became more available. It was the catalyst that enabled journalism to flourish as more stories could be written and read than at any time in history.

In the work I have done with executive teams, the ones that have been most impressive and visibly more organised and more successful are the ones that do the hard-smart work. The ones that do the analysis. Now while the term analysis is commonly used in business, there is much more to it than meets the eye.

---

28 Lienhard, op cit.
29 Dunlap, David W. (2014, November 13). "1978: Farewell, Etaoin Shrdlu." *The New York Times.* Retrieved from: http://www.nytimes.com/times-insider/2014/11/13/1978-farewell-etaoin-shrdlu/?_r=0

There are hundreds of ways to analyse, from highly quantifiable analysis using Monte Carlo simulation or Bayesian Networks through to simple stakeholder analysis. Personally I like a range of tools. Why? Because analysis addresses a key risk in your decision-making process. It addresses the risk that you don't know nearly enough about key issues like market drivers, implementation challenges and/or your organisation's capacity to deliver.

When you go to a physiotherapist about a back problem they treat you with what they learnt in their physiotherapy course. Go to a chiropractor and they treat you with what they learnt in their chiropractor course. It may be the same ailment, but if you consult an acupuncturist they treat you in another entirely different way. What is wrong with this picture? If you only have a hammer, everything is a nail to you. While obviously each of these professions have success, it makes sense that a combination of approaches is better than just using the one tool. Wouldn't it be better to go to someone who had mastery of all those skills?

The reason this sort of Nirvana does not exist is because of the time and effort required to become an expert in one field, let alone all of them. However, it illustrates my point. Don't hit everything you come across with a hammer. Have a good think about what you are trying to clarify, what you are trying to achieve and choose an appropriate set of tools to help you. If you don't you may find yourself saying one day, "If I had known that I wouldn't have …"

Options

Despite doing the hard-smart work, knowing precisely what to do and how to do it isn't simple or the norm. The complexity can range from subtle to mind boggling. Just because you have been working in the industry for 20 years, you know everyone there is to know and you "have seen it all", doesn't mean you know it all. It doesn't even mean you know enough. The world is constantly changing and even tried and tested business strategies can be becoming obsolete right under your nose. Think IBM and the personal computer versus the mainframe; Kodak film and print photographs versus digital photography; Microsoft's focus on software versus Apple's focus on devices, and the big credit-card companies and the advent of PayPal. In this modern world big businesses are being disrupted by more agile start-ups. Medium-sized businesses are being squeezed. Now is not the time to be complacent.

In order to make the best decision on your next step, what you should be looking for is options. But how many options should you be considering? Too many can create confusion and be a cause of feeling overwhelmed. On the other hand, you need enough options to ensure that you have good ones to choose from. What's important is that you have the time to give proper consideration to each of the options presented. The trouble is, people tend to be blinkered in the development of options.

Research. What would you do to develop your options if you were a hard-smart thinking manager? You would focus a significant portion of your attention on research. Research is key to the development of options. And I don't mean researching with the hammer you used last time. You must move away from same same. Sending a questionnaire to your customer base with the usual questions will do a pretty good job of reinforcing your current thinking. Setting ambitious objectives for your research and using a variety of methods will provide different results. Where would Apple be if Steve Jobs hadn't designed something we did not even know we wanted? And boy, didn't we want the iPhone and the iPad badly?

One of the most telling lessons of lack of research and how we limit our options is told by Ernesto Sirolli. Sirolli worked for an Italian non-government organisation, or NGO, delivering aid-funded projects into Africa. In his TED Talk called, "Want to help someone? Shut up and listen!", he openly states that every one of their projects failed.[30] He tells an amusing story of "teaching" Zambians to grow tomatoes and zucchinis. He and his colleagues couldn't understand why there was no agriculture in the lush valley and they earnestly set about to show the Zambians how fertile their land was. The tomatoes were growing huge and lush. Then one night, out of the river came a large herd of hippos and ate the lot. And that is when Sirolli and his colleagues learnt why the Zambians did not have any agriculture in their valley. When they asked the Zambians why they hadn't told them about the hippos, the answer was, "You never asked".

---

30 "Ernesto Sirolli (2012). Want to Help Someone? Shut Up and Listen!
TED. com. From: https://www.ted.com/talks/ernesto_sirolli_want_to_help_someone_
shut_up_and_listen/transcript

Sirolli goes on to make the point that western aid providers thought they knew what was best for Africa and that some US$2 trillion of aid was wasted because NGOs and other aid organisations didn't listen. To state the obvious, it is not just aid providers that have this problem.

Stakeholders. I should let you in on another secret. Where we do our listening is incredibly important. People will talk more openly and candidly in a café than in a meeting with the older, more experienced and more learned management team. You want to know what is being talked about at the water cooler. You want to know what people think. How many times have you seen a senior manager announce a commitment to a new project when the majority of staff think the goal is impossible to reach, or simply not in keeping with what they believe are the values of the organisation? Now I know there are great leaders who can set an incredible vision and create an atmosphere where teams are able to make the seemingly impossible, possible. However, you had better make sure you have done the hard-smart work to know how you are going to do it.

It is not just listening to people. It's listening to the right people. Sirolli has identified that for community projects to work, entrepreneurs are required. And, as he says in his TED Talk, entrepreneurs don't come to community meetings and unveil their great ideas to everyone. You have so seek out the entrepreneurs in your organisation.

Diversity. Like the hammer holder who sees everything as a nail, executives are blinded to all the options by their background. Let me explain. If you are a finance person you will likely first look at a problem from a finance perspective, and think something along the lines "the cost base is too high". If a marketing person, you look at things from a marketing perspective: "the branding is all wrong". We are too narrow in our focus.

The most successful management teams are those that develop the best suite of options. They don't rely on research and consultation alone; they also ensure diversity on their team. In September 2013, Australians elected a conservative government with Tony Abbott as prime minister. In his first Cabinet he appointed only one woman. One out of 19 cabinet positions went to a woman. There was widespread public outcry. Abbott responded that the appointments were based on merit and that there were many good women coming through the ranks.

In the following 18 months the Abbott government played some very hard lines. Its first budget in May 2014 was widely regarded as extremely hard on the most needy in Australian society. Treasurer Joe Hockey and Finance Minister Mathias Cormann were filmed smoking cigars in the lead-up to delivering the budget and the headlines and the social media traffic were damning as the budget leaks told a bleak story. Labels like "Fat Cats" and headlines like "Our dreams going up in smoke" were rampant.

After the budget the government had a hard time selling it. Calls of "gaffe" and "lack of understanding of the common people" from a broad range of think tanks and well respected social commentators abounded. Things got worse for Abbott. He became infamous for his "Captain's Calls". His most noted was his decision to award Prince Phillip Australia's highest honour, a Knighthood of the Order of Australia. The background is that Prince Phillip is the husband of Queen Elizabeth, Australia's head of state. Many in Australia would like to see an Australian as head of state, and many were incensed that Abbott had not only reinstated the honours but that he had awarded Prince Phillip, the same man that on a 2002 visit to Australia asked an indigenous person, "Do you still throw spears at each other?"

There had already been significant malcontent among the outer ministry and backbenchers about a lack of consultation and lack of access to the prime minister. Eventually, there was a "party room" meeting of all elected members to vote on whether the prime minister should allow a spill to be called, or in other words, allow his position to be contested. The motion was defeated, however, much damage was done. Abbott said he would change; that there would be less captain's calls and more consultation with colleagues.

Once the cracks appear, it is easy for the media to find more faults. Not long after the spill motion, Abbott was commenting on the Western Australia Government's plans to close half of that state's remote indigenous communities due to the cost of providing the services, such as schools and medical clinics. Abbott was recorded on TV as saying, "What we can't do is endlessly subsidise lifestyle choices if those lifestyle choices are not conducive to the kind of full participation in Australian society that everyone should have."[31] This was widely interpreted and reported as Abbott saying that indigenous people live where they live as a lifestyle choice; as Abbott having little appreciation of Aboriginal culture and history.

Abbott and his government were coming through loud and clear as hardliners.

Who shone through during this period? Foreign Affairs Minister Julie Bishop. The lone woman in cabinet. When she subsequently publicly showed displeasure at the possibility of a reduction in Australia's foreign-aid budget, the treasurer was quick to assure her the budget was safe. Her influence had grown markedly in recent months.

After surviving the leadership-spill motion, Abbott asked for six months to show he could change. But, seven months later he was ousted in a leadership challenge brought by Malcolm Turnbull.

Let me leave the final word on the benefits of diversity to Ernesto Sirolli. In his TED Talk, he refers to teaching entrepreneurship and he explains how he starts by asking the class to read the first two pages of Richard Branson's autobiography and to count how many more times Branson uses "we" than he does "I". The answer is 32. Branson also states multiple times that no one starts a company alone.

---

31 From: http://www.abc.net.au/news/2015-03-10/tony-abbott-backs-decision-to-close-wa-indigenous-communities/6295296

By now, I am sure you are as convinced as I am, that multiple heads are better than one when clarifying the options from which you are going to choose when you make your decision. Of course, not only multiple heads, but diverse ones as well. Remember the earlier discussion on group think and the Bay of Pigs. So what else is at risk in our decision making?

Creativity. I started this chapter on clarifying your decision making by discussing hard-smart work. Well there is one more step you need to take. It's a step many leaders and executives ignore. And that is developing brand new options that you have never even conceived of before. That takes commitment and that is why only the hardest, smartest hard-smart workers do it. How do they do it? With creative thinking.

A lot of creative thinking is driven by naturally creative people who will not accept the norm. It's leaders with a vision like Bill Gates and Steve Jobs, where the only "option" was to do something different, something exciting. Not all of us are blessed with these visions or leadership skills and so the mere mortals among us have to get some help. My help came from reading the works of one of the fathers of creative thinking, Edward de Bono. From my experience, creative thinking techniques open people's eyes at just the right time in their deliberations and they are much, much more open to other possibilities.

A simple example is de Bono's creative thinking technique, which he calls "focus". This is where you break a problem down into smaller and smaller bits and focus on each element, thinking about what it means to the problem and how you might do something differently. I started using the technique when facilitating risk workshops in the 1990s. I would ask the team to develop a work breakdown structure for a project, or a process flow map for a process they were assessing the risk of. I would then ask them to focus in on each component. It escalated dramatically the issues each team would find. Better still, more often than not, it identified better options for project delivery or process design the team had not yet thought of. The process itself helped focus thinking, visualise scenarios, elicit new options and strategies. A realm of opportunity opened up.

Developing a good suite of options is one of the most overlooked elements of decision making. You just need to do the hard-smart work.

Real options

What does an interchange bench or a reserve bench do for a team in sport? It provides the coach with options, real options, depending on how the game plays out. If a player is injured, a reserve bench provides the coach with a range of players to choose from and that is why the bench is often frequented by great all-round performers, players who can carry out a range of roles.

In the game of rugby league, which is not very well known outside of a handful of countries, the interchange bench is used to both cover injuries and to take advantage of opportunities.

Rugby league is played with 13 players a side. It is a tough hard game requiring strength and fitness. Much of the game is played out with the big players on one team looking to dominate the big players on the other team so the smaller, more agile players can take advantage of the tired, dominated group and run amok. Late in a game, irrespective of whether one team has been able to dominate the other, opportunities arise for fresh players to come on to the playing field and take advantage of tired players all over the field. In essence, this is a coach exercising what has become known in the business world as exercising a "real option".

The understanding that real options are a source of competitive advantage in business arose as our understanding of the financial instruments known as "options" increased in the last quarter of the last century. Options are financial instruments, which in their simplest terms are bets by one party with another party as to the future market price of an underlying tradeable commodity such as the US dollar or company shares. In 1973, the Black-Scholes model was introduced. It combined trading strategies broadly referred to as "hedges", and led to the concept of dealing with future uncertainty by buying certainty today. That is, you might hedge the risk posed to your business by a sharp movement in the price of oil by taking out an option to buy a certain amount of the commodity at a certain price in the future.

Let's look at a foreign-exchange example. If you are in France and supplying your products to the Middle East and all your contracts are in US dollars, there is a risk that after you agree on the price for the contract, the value of the dollar against the Euro decreases. Hence, when you are paid in the future, the value of the work you have performed or the products you have produced has decreased from today because you are paid less than when you signed the contract. You are caught short. Through a hedging strategy you are able to reduce or eliminate that risk. However, you have to pay for that privilege, the same as you pay an insurance company an insurance premium to take on your risk of damage to your car. You pay a counterparty to take that risk for you. They take that risk as a core process of their business and they manage that risk through a range of strategies. This enables them to charge you a reasonable "premium" for you to relieve yourself of the burden of the risk of adverse movement of the currency.

The field of so-called real options is about valuing an option to defer a decision in part or in full. For example, you may be trying to decide between a minor expansion, a major expansion or no expansion of your factory. A standard approach to looking at these options and making a decision is to calculate the NPV (net present value) for each and choosing the one with the best return. The field of real options asks you to use a different valuation methodology. As an example, it asks you to consider the value of the option that an expanded facility provides, that is the option of having the flexibility of increasing production if you need it. We all know an NPV calculation depends on assumptions about the future demand for our product and that predicting the future is not possible. Real options bring in the reality that you are most likely going to be somewhat wrong and using methods such as Black-Scholes, you are able to value the flexibility an expansion option provides.

I am not going to go into the detail of real options here as entire books have been written on the subject. However, I do wish to leave you with this quote from the author of a book I read on real options: "It seems we must live with risk; and if we must, it's best to enjoy the ride." A wonderful line by F. Peter Boer in his book *The Real Options Solution*.[32] It reminded me that great minds across so many disciplines have been grappling for decades with the challenge that risk poses to our decision making and that dealing with that risk is fundamental to our success.

Outcomes

Most decisions are not about binary outcomes, yes or no, one or zero, $100 million and so on. Most outcomes can be placed on a continuum from terribly bad, through bad, mediocre, good, very good, through to great. So when someone is presenting to you a business case, such as to build a new plant or not, you actually have a range of outcomes to consider. The new plant could be a dud, mediocre, successful or hugely successful. Outcomes are more often than not on a continuum.

---

32 Boer, F. Peter (2002). *The Real Options Solution: Finding Total Value in a High-Risk World*, Wiley, N.Y.

In addition to outcomes being on a continuum, any point on that continuum has a likelihood, probably a-difficult-to-estimate likelihood, of occurring. Remember, anything is possible.

What does this mean? This all points to the advantages of risk-based decision making. Assign a likelihood to number of points on the outcome continuum. Each point should be as well researched and analysed as needs be for the importance of the decision and the availability of information. Not by simply using your gut-feel. The gut-feel trap has been proven by many researchers. Now you are in a position to make a more informed decision as you can see a bigger picture of the potential upside and downside for the project.

A perfect example of how this works for decision makers involves the insurance industry. Why do we buy insurance? Because of the burden of risk. The thought about the pain we will suffer if we lost our family home to fire drives us to transfer the risk to an insurance company in exchange for a fee called a premium. While this fee sometimes feels exorbitant, we still pay because the alternative is so unpalatable. When we transfer our burden on to the insurance company something happens that most of us don't appreciate. We create a burden of risk for the insurance company.

The insurance company's burden of risk is that they cannot be certain how many of the people they insure will claim and how much they will claim in any given period of time. That is, the potential claims are on quite a broad continuum from where the company can make super profits through to where all of the company's capital is used up and the insurer is insolvent. The board and management of insurance companies have a decision to make. How much capital should they keep? The less capital they keep, the better their return on capital employed when all goes well. On the flip side, the greater is the risk they could, on relatively rare occasions such as the Christchurch earthquakes, run out of capital to pay claims and become insolvent. The victims become the poor people who can't get their claims paid, the shareholders and the insurer's suppliers. Because of the potential impact this has on society, governments around the world regulate the amount of capital insurance companies must keep for the rare occasions when claims are much worse than the average. One can look at the 2001 collapse of HIH Insurance in Australia to see the grief and chaos caused when an insurer goes into liquidation.

Why do we need governments to regulate insurance companies? Think about the decision makers, who influences them, what is motivating them? Remember, the first step in managing the risk to our decision making is to understand what is motivating us.

The decision makers in an insurance company are ultimately the directors on the board. Management is the chief influencer. Insurance companies in free market economies are there to make profits. In order to be competitive they need to price competitively. They also need capital from investors so they can offer insurance policies. Investors need an adequate return on their investment for the risk they take.

Hence they want decisions made to maximise the return on capital employed.

The big problem facing the insurance industry, particularly in a smaller economies like Australia or New Zealand, is the market is very competitive. While insurance company bashing is often a favourite activity of the public and the media, the truth is that insurance companies only make extra large returns on capital in very few years out of 10. The norm is a less than exciting return for the risk being taken. While there is strong competition, prices are suppressed and the amount of cash the insurers are collecting to pay claims is increasingly skinny by comparison with the better years. Then lo and behold along comes a bad year for claims and the losses mount. The market then corrects pricing and outcries from the public start afresh as prices double overnight. As prices double, fresh capital comes in to take advantage and the downward pressure on pricing starts again.

Enough of my lecture on the vagaries of the insurance market and back to some insight on the continuum of outcomes from a decision, and how the insurance industry handles it. They hire actuaries. Actuaries build sophisticated statistical models that predict the likelihood of the outcomes of a year of claims across a continuum called a probability distribution. As an example, for any particular line of business, such as residential home and contents insurance, the expected claims might be estimated to be between $100 million and $150 million in nine out of 10 years, that is 90 percent of the time. However, the probability distribution at the tail end of the curve, say the bad end, might indicate claims could be $175 million once every 20 years, $200 million once every 50 years, $300 million once every 100 years and $500 million once every 1,000 years.

So if you were the leader of an insurance company, how much capital would you hold for the same amount of expected income, year on year? The answer insurance leaders have given over the years varies considerably. Some have been more conservative than others. Why would all leaders make the same decision when we all have different motivations and different views of the clarity of the risk being taken? Consequently, the result has been that insurance companies across the globe have gone bust from time to time.

The response of regulators has been to set minimum capital requirements for insurers that wish to offer insurance in their market. By setting a minimum, it puts all players on a much more level playing field from which they can then compete. It essentially puts a floor under the price that can be charged for insurance in a market and should, at least in theory, stop insurers pricing irrationally for extended periods of time as was the case in the lead up to the collapse of HIH in Australia.

Insurance companies and their actuaries have the luxury of a lot of data for their sophisticated models, and the benefits cannot be ignored. If we were to take a leaf out of their book and apply it to the decisions you are making in your business on any given day, week, month or year, how would it help you improve your decision making? What would you learn?

Here is a tip. When you are considering a decision, think of how it might end up if it goes really well, and keep thinking of different scenarios along the continuum, through to really bad. Get yourself say five different results. Then write down beside them the likelihood of each one occurring from 0 chance to 100 percent likely.

Now you have a very valuable tool for decision making. First, you can use it to look at the worst case so you can decide if you can survive the worst case, that is the one-in-a-thousand bad outcome. This may or may not be important to you, depending on the drivers of your decision. However, for most business people, rule number one is "don't bite off more than you can chew".

Second, you can do the same thing for a range of options. For example, you may be deciding between investing in a major expansion to your factory, a minor expansion or no expansion. Each decision will have a different probability distribution of a profit outcome depending on what your assumptions are for where the market is heading. Completing the exercise for each option allows for a clearer comparison. It might show that the potential difference in profit between one and another is simply not worth the risk, or it might show very clearly that you can afford the downside in all cases and the upside is too good to be missed.

While you might do exactly this in a more sophisticated way when building a robust business case, how about all of those other decisions you are making? How long did it take you to think about the outcomes, their probabilities and to draw up the graph? How many decisions did you make last year that you might have made differently if you had of taken the time to write down the range of outcomes for each option and their likelihood of occurring?

From here on in, if you have not already trained yourself to do so, thinking about every decision resulting in a range of outcomes must become part of your decision-making discipline.

Chapter 8

Clarification Traps

Despite our best intentions to do the hard-smart work, to develop a good range of options and to think about the continuum of outcomes that can result, we can still fall into a range of traps. This chapter discusses a few key ones that are related to, but different to, the core set of psychological biases I discussed earlier. They are ones I see happening all the time when decisions are being made. They are worthy of bringing to your attention. Let's start with one that has a terrifically Australian flavour to it.

'She'll be right' attitudes

In Australia we have a great saying, "She'll be right". It means the same as the actor who says, "Don't worry, it will be alright on the night". It is a very powerful tool for relaxing people, for taking the pressure off. Let it pervade your decision making, however, and you have fallen for a trap. You need to think clearly when to use it and when not to. You need to consider the risk. Is this a case of you falling right into decision-trap, or is it a perfect time to relax you and your team so that the implementation decisions are not adversely affected by too much pressure?

Australia's third longest-serving prime minister, Bob Hawke, led the country from 1983 until 1991. He had a reputation as being more of a regular guy than any before or since him. He made people laugh and he said unstatesmanlike things such as, "Any boss who sacks anyone for not turning up today is a bum." Hawke said this following the inspiring America's Cup yacht race win by Australia II in 1983. A lot of people across the nation were awake in the wee hours of the morning watching the seventh and final race of the world's most famous sailing race. The US had held the cup and had defeated all comers for 132 years and it was a moment of intense pride and joy for Australia. And then the partying began.

Hawke certainly had a "she'll-be-right" attitude. However, for the most part he used it wisely. He fought hard for workers' issues while balancing those concerns against big business issues. He implemented a compulsory employer-paid superannuation scheme for workers. He also deregulated the financial sector and floated the Australian dollar, putting his faith in market economics.

So what was Hawke thinking as Australia's 1988 bicentennial celebrations approached? The celebration of the beginning of European settlement in Australia. An event seen as an invasion by the indigenous people of Australia. In 1980, before Hawke became prime minister, the Australian Bicentennial Authority was created through an Act of Parliament. Its mission was to find a way to celebrate the bicentenary with sensitivity while building a stronger sense of what being Australian really meant. The leaders of the authority decided the celebration "should be seen as a day of contact, not of conquest ... the day which began the fusion of Australians".[33]

In the lead up to the celebrations, while many recognised the extreme sensitivity of the indigenous population who had suffered terribly at the hands of the Europeans, not all were so inclined. In an article published by the Institute of Public Affairs in 1985, Dr Ken Baker strongly questioned whether the plans established by the authority was heading Australia down the path of an apology rather than a celebration.[34] Baker argued, "How we choose to celebrate it should reflect the pride most Australians feel about their country."

Hawke was also known as a consensus leader. He worked hard to find the middle ground so that all parties could support the direction chosen. The consensus challenge for the bicentennial celebrations proved a challenging one indeed.

As Australia Day, January 26, 1988 drew nearer, the indigenous community was rallying behind their own theme. The 26th of

---

33 From: http://www.australiaday.org.au/australia-day/history/1988-the-bicentenary/ accessed 22/03/2015.

34 Baker, Ken (1985). "The Bicentenary: celebration or apology?" *IPA Review* 38.4, pp 175-182.

January 1788 was Invasion Day, not a day of celebration. As momentum built for Invasion Day, the Hawke Government realised the delicate balance needed for the event. For example, the government was against the privately organised and funded re-enactment of the First Fleet entering Sydney Harbour because of insensitivity towards indigenous people. This created more challenges for Hawke as this position reportedly incensed Australia's head of state, Queen Elizabeth II of England.[35]

What transpired has been captured in a documentary called, simply, "88" written by Adrian Russell Wills and Michaela Perske.[36] It tells the tale of the indigenous community travelling thousands of kilometres by mini-bus, truck and car and meeting up in a town near Sydney in preparation for a convoy of protest into Sydney. It is a compelling story. The convoy was not met with disdain or policy barriers, it was met with respect and recognition. While on the one hand there was much to celebrate, most Australians knew that what the placards said was true: "White Australia has a black history".[37]

Why then did Bob Hawke's Bicentennial Australia Day speech not mention the indigenous people of Australia? He

35 Tanner, Richard J. (2010, Jan. 26). The First Fleet and the Re-enactment First Fleet : Some Historical Parallels and Differences. Address presented to The Order of Australia Association. NSW Branch. Australia Day Event. Retrieved from http://www.theorderofaustralia.asn.au/downloads/NSWRJTAddressJan10_000.pdf

36 From: http://www.smh.com.au/entertainment/tv-and-radio/88-20140122-317ff.html

37 From: http://www.australiaday.org.au/australia-day/history/1988-the-bicentenary/

would have been well aware of the convoy protesting Invasion Day. Whatever his deepest thoughts he must surely have said to himself "she'll be right" and gone on to deliver the speech many Australians wanted. When you watch "88" today, after the efforts at reconciliation between white and indigenous Australia, you cannot help but say to yourself, "What was he thinking?"

My advice when it comes to playing the "she'll be right" card is to ask yourself, "Are people worrying unnecessarily?" If so, relieve the pressure.

Very rare, very big, very nasty events

Since Charles Darwin's *Origin of Species,* we have recognised how nature adapts to survive. As humans we seemed to have evolved while following a common process. We try something new. If it hurts us we learn and take action in proportion to the degree of pain. The next time we face the same pain we are better prepared and we go back for more, and either avoid the pain or find a way of working to a new pain threshold.

It appears the more frequent the pain, the faster we learn, the quicker we adapt. The less frequent the pain, the slower we learn. In corporate life, the pain that throbs strongest in the corporate memory is the pain we work hardest to avoid. Take the process Disney follows to avoid being sued for breach of intellectual property.

A colleague told me he wrote a book and sent it to Disney suggesting to them it could be the basis of a great movie. They sent it back unopened with a letter from their lawyers saying they did not open it and won't read it – full stop. My colleague since learned that early on Walt Disney had been sued for breach of copyright. Because of that experience, Walt and subsequent leaders of Disney have made sure it is one risk that is burned deeply into the corporate memory.

Irrespective of your corporate history, events can repeat themselves because the really big lessons have very long periods of time between them and they are simply forgotten. That is, we fail to take into account highly unlikely events. We simply don't even consider them. My suggestion to you is that when you are considering the potential outcomes of a decision that is much more important than usual, such as most strategic decisions, take time to consider the highly improbable. Not because I want you to worry, not because I want to tie you up in knots trying to think through a decision, it is because sometimes there are some very simple things you can do to deal with that highly improbable outcome to take it to zero or near-zero probability.

A technique first introduced by Gary Klein called a premortem is a valuable tool for this kind of analysis.[38] Go to the end of the outcome continuum we discussed earlier, take the near impossible bad outcome and work backwards identifying each event so you can make sure the unwanted

---

38 Klein, G (2003). *Intuition at Work: Why Developing Your Gut Instincts Will Make You Better at What You Do*. Currency Doubleday, N.Y.

events do not occur or you are prepared for them if they are outside of your control.

Despite this type of thinking, there are still rarer and nastier events that we have trouble getting our minds around so we tend to leave them out of our decision making. For example, a meteorite hitting a city of three million people where your main manufacturing site is located. Of course we discount such an event. We will have many more things to worry about as a planet if a meteorite destroys much of a city of three million people.

The question we must therefore ask ourselves is, "What is a credible scenario?" How bad could it really be? Take the BP oil spill in the Gulf of Mexico. When the US authorities approved deep sea drilling, did they know there was no guarantee a well blowout could be stopped in a timely and orderly manner? At the very least they would have known that there was no proven methods as it had never had to be done before. Should they have covered this more diligently than they did? With the benefit of Harry Hindsight it is easy to say yes. Having made the odd mistake in my life, I won't be the first to throw stones. What I will say is that perhaps if they had done more of the hard-smart work that good decision making requires, they may have drawn different conclusions and set more rigorous requirements for oil companies to fulfil before allowing deep sea drilling.

Despite events such as the BP oil spill, we still have trouble thinking past the highly unlikely and into the realm of very rare, very big, very nasty events. Someone who has given a name to these things and provided a way for us to move forward is Nassim Nicholas Taleb, author of *The Black Swan, The Impact of the Highly Improbable*.[39]

Taleb argues that some things simply cannot be predicted so don't try to. The example he uses is the black swan. Prior to the first visits of non-indigenous people to the land now known as Australia, there was nothing in the non-indigenous person's concept of a swan that would lead them to think of a black swan. Why? Because black swans only exist in Australia. So you can well imagine when Dutch explorer Dirk Hartog came across the west coast of Australia in 1616 that it was highly unlikely he would turn to his second in command and say, "I bet you a 'gulden' that when we get off this ship we will find a black swan." The thought would have been ludicrous.

What lessons does Taleb take from this knowledge that despite what you want to believe, some things can go wrong no matter how well you have planned them? His tip is always have something in reserve. This type of thinking is a core element of sound decision making and I like to cover it off with the old saying, "Remember rule number one!" For me, rule number one of decision making is: "Never bite off more than you can chew". I follow this up closely with rule number two which is: "Only break rule number one if you have no other choice." In the case where our key motivation is survival, we may have no

---

39 Nassim Nicholas Taleb (2007). *The Black Swan: The Impact of the Highly Improbable*. Random House, N.Y.

other option but to try something that is even highly uncertain as our only hope of survival.

Before I leave this section I want to touch on society's approach to climate change. While nothing in this world seems entirely certain except for "death and taxes", every now and then one has to face the prospect of an uncertain and potentially horrific outcome. One we might be able to do something about although we don't really want to because it would be inconvenient and difficult. Think give up smoking or alcohol.

In 2012, I was asked to facilitate a session for the Risk Management Institution of Australasia on the risks associated with climate change and the proposed carbon tax of the Australian Government at the time. One of my great learnings from the session was thanks to one of the participants. He recalled to me Pascal's Wager.

Pascal's Wager was 17th century philosopher Blaise Pascal's way of thinking about a truly difficult conundrum for him: "Should I believe in God?" He thought about it as a wager where the stakes were extreme – heaven versus hell.

I've captured Pascal's Wager in Table 3 below. Irrespective of one's position on the existence of God, Pascal's Wager certainly shows that the stakes can be seen as extreme.

Table 3: Pascal's Wager

	God exists	God does not exist
Believe in God	Heaven for eternity	A good time wasted
Disbelieve in God	Hell for eternity	No matter

Similarly, given some of the dire predictions, the stakes can be seen as extreme in the climate change and carbon tax debates.

In the table below I've portrayed Pascal's Wager for climate change. You will see from this simple analysis, the stakes are indeed potentially extreme for the key stakeholders as these issues literally have the potential to impact political careers, the overall economic wellbeing of our society and matters of life and death.

Table 4: Pascal's Wager – Climate Change

	Humans are causing damaging climate change	Humans are not affecting the climate
Combat climate change	Avert economic and social disaster	Opportunity lost to use resources for whatever we wanted
Do not combat climate change	Economic and social disaster	No matter

What I found about Pascal's Wager and applying it to these two issues, is that it puts very rare, very big, very nasty events into perspective. It is then up to informed decision making to take over, to apply some likelihoods to the outcomes in ranges. This will guide how much effort we put into addressing climate change and how quickly.

I think Rupert Murdoch, chairman and CEO of News Corp., summed it up best when considering the climate change debate, he said, "The planet deserves the benefit of the doubt."

Analysis phobias

I have long been an advocate of quantifying everything that you can. It's simpler that way. If you are a private sector for-profit organisation, it is easier to make a case one way or another for an idea if you can bring it down to how it will affect the bottom-line. In government or not-for-profit, if you can compare numbers it reduces the subjectivity enormously. When I dwell on this subject I am reminded of the countless workshops I have facilitated where someone makes a statement along the lines of, "that is not likely to happen" having simply plucked their answer out of thin air. I have been advocating government, for example, to collect information so that numbers can be derived for the likelihood of the outcomes of policy and other decisions.

Unfortunately many people are scared of numbers or are anti-measurement. They are the ones saying, "that is impossible to measure". I will give you one example where an industry was forced to face that myth. It's from the chemical and related process industry.

As the chemical industry became bigger and more ambitious in the second half of last century, so did the size and scale of the disasters it caused. From the Flixborough explosion in England which killed 28 people in 1974 to the toxic gas leak in Bophal, India that killed thousands of people in 1984, the trend was alarming. Eventually the authorities stepped in and said to the industry, "If you want to grow your business or even stay in business, you need to show us you can do it safely." How do you show you can operate safely? You must do so via objective measures.

With the challenge quite rightly posed by regulators, the industry started working on ways to show that their plants were safe or could be made to be safe through additional control measures. The key objective measure was the risk any individual plant posed to the public. The aim was to show that the background risk to the public was acceptable by comparing the risk to other risks the population already faces, such as the risk taken in driving a car or taking a plane or the risk of being struck by lightning.

The industry was able to work with others to access data on the background level of risk taken by the public in general. For example they delved into the decades of government statistics about road accidents. That was the easy part. The hard part was gathering the data on their own accident rates.

The industry began working on collecting the data, analysing it and coming up with credible statistics such as the number of high-pressure gas leaks per kilometre of pipe per year given the size of the pipe and the pressure it was containing. The industry also started building computer models to help process the data from different data sources. For example, if there was a gas leak, what is the likelihood the wind would be blowing in a particular direction? How strong would the wind be? How fast would a particular gas disperse at that wind speed if it was a hot day or a cold night? Data from the weather bureau had to be processed along with the industry's data.

The long and the short of it is that despite the huge growth in demand for what the chemical and related process industries produce, the industry's safety record has been improving. While we still hear of disasters such as the fertilizer plant explosion in the town of West, Texas in 2013, which killed 15, the number of incidents compared with the amount of chemicals that are being produced continues to reduce. The chemical industry has shown it can be done.

I would not be a realist if I did not observe that the chemical and related industries are full of engineers like myself who are not afraid of numbers. Hence the challenge remains a significant one when moving into business. One measurement evangelist I have come to admire through his books and other writings is Douglas Hubbard. While I certainly don't agree with everything he says, I do like his base mantra which is that anything can be measured. He rightly identifies the bigger questions: are you trying to measure the right things? and, what is the value you will gain versus the cost?

In his book *How to Measure Anything*, Hubbard remarks that if we had perfect information we would always make the right decision.[40] So the value of information is the difference between the outcome we would have reached if we had made the right decision and the value from the outcome we actually reached. He takes his time explaining to the reader how anything can be measured if you are asking the right question, that is if you know what decision you need to make. While recognising that many measurements rely on estimates of likelihood of outcomes

---

40 Hubbard, D (2010). *How to Measure Anything*. Second ed., Wiley, N.Y.

because there's insufficient data for a thorough analysis, Hubbard makes the case that experts can improve their ability to estimate likelihood and to overcome their psychological biases through calibration techniques. This is where experts are given estimating exercises to find how over or under confident they are so they can compensate and improve their estimates. After all, experts want to be right, not proven wrong down the track and lose their "expert" tag.

Another measurement evangelist is Ronny Kohavi of Microsoft. In a slight contrast to Hubbard, Kohavi urges: stop trying to estimate, stop arguing over the range estimate. Kohavi says go get the data. Now given he used to be director of data mining and personalization at Amazon.com[41], you might be excused for thinking, "Well it's easy for Microsoft or Amazon isn't it?" The question I think you should ask yourself is, "Do I have analysis phobia?" Have you really thought about the decision you want to make, what information you need to make it and thought through all the various ways you could get that information? Don't knock it until you have tried it.

Perceive first, ask questions later

While I have, on the one hand suggested that we should take more time to look for and understand the rarer, bigger and nastier events, there are times when a focus on the extreme can

---

41 Schrage, M (2015). Embrace your ignorance. *MIT Sloan management review*, *56*(2), pp. 95-96.

lead to poor decision making. This was highlighted in articles published in the newsletter of the Macquarie University Natural Hazard Research Group, Risk Frontiers.

These articles concerned the six Italian scientists and a government official who were found guilty of manslaughter for "failing to adequately communicate the level of risk" regarding an earthquake that killed 309 people in the Italian city of L'Aquila in April 2009. This group of men were all members of the National Commission for the Forecast and Prevention of Major Risks and were tasked with advising the public of the risk posed to the best of their ability. This is a difficult task as there is no known, or at least scientifically proven, method of predicting earthquakes to any great degree of accuracy.

On the one hand, author Koschatsky[42] believed the scientists involved allowed their scientific findings to be intentionally used to calm the public after a number of earthquake swarms and a prediction by one scientist of an imminent event. Marzocchi and Cocco[43] argued that the risk was not downplayed or underestimated and that it is difficult to communicate the risk of rare events. They argue that a focus on the worst-case scenario in a low-likelihood environment, which is often the least well understood in terms of outcomes, is to seek the

---

42 Koschatsky, V., Haynes K., Somerville P., McAneney J. & McAneney D. (2012), "Guilty?", *Risk Frontiers* Quarterly Newsletter, Natural Hazard Research Group, Macquarie University, Sydney. See: www.riskfrontiers.com/newsletters.html

43 Cocco, M and Marzocchi, W (June 2013), *Risk Frontiers* Quarterly Newsletter, Natural Hazard Research Group, vol. 13, issue 1. Macquarie University, Sydney. See: www.riskfrontiers.com/newsletters.html

avoidance of liability rather than a reasoned assessment of the range of outcomes to facilitate decision making. In terms of communicating the risk of low-likelihood events, they use the example of when a risk of something killing you has been identified as having a 10 percent chance of occurring, it is easy to get people to take it seriously. Whereas something that shifts the likelihood of killing you from 0.0001 percent to 0.01 percent, an increase in risk of 100 times, is not as likely to be taken as seriously. Certainly a vexing problem for advisers of decision makers.

Peter Sandman is to me the father of risk communication. I was first introduced to his work in the mid-1990s. Today on his website he leads with "Risk = Hazard + Outrage" meaning that the true risk level is the calculated risk level plus the emotions people attach to their interpretation of that risk. As an example, when we hear on the news that asbestos has been found in a school, we are concerned. We may even be concerned enough to comment that the authorities should be doing something about it. Now put yourself in the shoes of a parent with a child in that school. The risk level is now applied personally and the outrage builds and you want an immediate response, irrespective of the cost to whomever. "It is about my child!"

One of the problems you have in making your decisions is that you may not put yourself in the shoes of others to sufficiently understand how they might view the decision outcome you wish to pursue. To put it another way, you might underestimate how well you will be able to communicate risk. Sandman breaks up risk communication into four sectors he calls precautionary advocacy, outrage management, crisis management and the best spot to be, the sweet spot. Precautionary advocacy is where you need to get people to consider more acutely a serious risk, while outrage management is where you need to calm down people who are over reacting. Crisis management is for when you have to manage outrage, when people have a right to be outraged. The sweet spot is about when the risk is not too great and accordingly there's a low outrage level. When next you are thinking about your outcome curve and how it might be perceived by others, you should be asking yourself if anywhere on the curve could be perceived as anything other than the sweet spot for your stakeholders. You might think it is the single most wonderful decision you have ever made, however, you might have missed a very important perception of others that will need to be managed.

As I was writing this chapter a most apt example sprung up courtesy of one of Australia's largest companies, food and liquor retailer, Woolworths. ANZAC Day is to Australians and New Zealanders what Remembrance Day is to most other nations from the Allied Forces of the First World War. While Remembrance Day marks the end of WWI, ANZAC Day commemorates the first time the fledgling nations of Australia and New Zealand fought under their own leadership, independent of mother Britain. It is celebrated on April 25 in tribute to the thousands of men and women who fought and died and the tens of thousands who were part of the horrific

Gallipoli Campaign that commenced on that day in 1915. While the popularity of ANZAC Day has waxed and waned over the past 100 years, the Australian and New Zealand people were strongly behind celebrating the 100-year anniversary.

In what surely must seem in hindsight a flawed decision, Woolworths ran an advertising campaign with the lines "Lest We Forget" and "Fresh in our Memories". Woolworths has for many years been using "The Fresh Food People" as its key slogan. The idea behind the ANZAC-inspired advertisement was to connect the slogan the supermarket giant had ingrained in people's minds through tens of millions of dollars of advertising to slogans of the ANZAC commemorations. Consumers made the connection alright and they were outraged. After a massive outcry from the public, Woolworths canned the advertisement and apologised.

Woolworths had failed to put itself in the shoes of the consumer. It hadn't really thought through how the message might be received. There was outrage that a publicly listed, for-profit, organisation was looking to cash-in on a day of mourning and remembrance. What would a bit of market research cost to get a sense of the emotional response to the planned advertisement? A tiny fraction of the cost of reputation damage to be sure.

In my experience the hardest part of business, and life, to get right is to understand how your communications and your actions may be perceived. You can have the best product, the most innovative service, the greatest minds in the business and the smartest strategy. However, without the ability to communicate clearly and to influence perceptions you have next to nothing. Remember, we all have a tendency to perceive first and ask questions later. That is why the old saying "Don't judge a book by its cover" is so important. Unfortunately most people don't adhere to it.

Technology and disruptive innovation

Technophobe, technocrat, tech savvy, techie? Are you one of these? If not, you are one of the 80 percent of people that are happy users of technology, but you don't live by it and you don't avoid it like the plague. You have had some wonderful experiences of technology and you have had plenty of frustrations. As a manager you have been disappointed many times by technology initiatives that ended up more costly than forecast, took longer than planned or failed to see the light of day. You also know that so much has been achieved by technology, and that those tech entrepreneurs are coming up with new ideas all the time, that you will need to get your mind around it.

Getting clarification of an opportunity that technology may bring is not always easy. Getting clarification on whether your industry is about to be disrupted, how, by whom and when is even more complex because almost by definition, if it is a true disruption, it has not been done before and no one, not even the disrupter is sure what it is going to look like.

What does it take to understand technology and its implications? First of all it takes education and this is our first and biggest failing. Last year I decided to help out my alma mater and attended what I would call a speed mentoring evening for young business school undergraduates. I did it partly because I wanted to help but also because I was interested to find out what was on the minds of young undergraduates these days.

What I learnt at the session was that these future leaders of business, the future CEOs, CFOs and COOs, were not being educated in technology, let alone the management of it. I mentioned my observations to a friend who works for EMC, a major technology provider, and he agreed it was a big problem. He then told me about a colleague of his that became CIO (chief information officer) at one of the major oil companies. His colleague had recently told him that all he seems to do these days is translate what the C-suite want into techie-speak and then translate back what the techies recommend into C-suite speak. Yes, the techies are guilty of not being able to communicate effectively and influence decision makers because they can't translate technology issues and benefits into business issues and benefits. However, aren't managers equally as guilty of not learning enough about technology to ask the right questions to make better informed decisions?

The number of organisations I have worked with where the CIO has been turned over more times than the reception desk is to me a sad indictment on the profession of management. And what was my old alma mater doing about it in undergraduate classes? Nothing. Zip.

That for me is the crux of the technology issue. The trap is you may have to rely too often on a technical specialist for advice because you haven't done enough to understand the fundamentals of technology management. That is, understanding what infrastructure is, what architecture means, what a service is and isn't in a techie's world. When next you are talking to a senior manager, ask them if they have a good understanding of the implications of a technology failure for their organisation and if they have made a conscious decision on how much to invest in ensuring it works now, next month, next year and beyond. Way too often I see organisations being hamstrung by years of under-investment in technology.

Now that I have covered issues to do with technology, I want to talk about industry disruption. The full-on industry disruption piece is a different trap. When I say disruption, I am thinking Google Adwords and newspaper advertising, Uber and the taxi industry, AirBnB and the hotel industry.

> In 2015 Uber, the world's largest taxi company owns no vehicles, Facebook the world's most popular media owner creates no content, Alibaba, the most valuable retailer has no inventory and Airbnb the world's largest accommodation provider owns no real estate.
>
> – Tom Goodwin, SVP Strategy and Innovation,
> Havas Media, published on LinkedIn.

Industry disruption is usually driven by a small agile startup with more than a penchant for innovative thinking, and overly excitable founders who find it hard to sleep at night as they are so excited about their idea they simply cannot wait to see it come into reality. Now turn and look at their intended target. What do you see? Traditional businesses that have gradually built resilience through building financial, market and internal strength. They have worked out what works to keep a good thing going. They innovate within the construct of their industry. That's where the trap is: inside the industry's self-created construct. It is not until someone asks themselves about the true purpose of their industry that they can begin to see how it could be vulnerable.

While the Intercontinental Hotel chain's Holiday Inn franchise may think the industry it is in is the hotel business, in a specific niche of running affordable and safe hotels for families to holiday in, Airbnb founders were thinking differently back in 2007 and 2008. I once saw an infographic by Anna Vital who mapped out the Airbnb story from when they rented out mattresses on their floor when accommodation demand was at its peak, through a basic website offering, through the sourcing of seed funding and its development into a serious business before it became a proven concept, became fully funded and it became the juggernaut it is today.

While the infographic told a great story, it only gave us an inkling of what the founders of Airbnb were thinking, so let me take a guess.

I think they were thinking about things like the cost of accommodation, about basic economics like supply and demand

and what was happening in the world with hotel booking sites like Wotif and online markets like eBay. As time wore on, they were able to make some money from the venture, focusing on supply versus demand when large conferences were on in San Francisco.

Since the rise of Airbnb, the traditional hotel industry has had to adapt. One great example is the need to monitor and manage online ratings of their establishments and their service which of course means that they have had to improve to compete. That service includes an emphasis on the safety of their guests. While most people love a great holiday, they put a higher priority on their safety. All in all, Airbnb has provided consumers with more options at more affordable prices with an emphasis on safety.

What should you do if you are one of the traditional organisations potentially exposed to disruption? I advise you to take a leaf out of Google's book and let your best and brightest have thinking or development time each week. Let them play and come up with the craziest of ideas. Filter those ideas and then provide direction and instill the courage to change to meet the disruption head on or to create a new destiny for your organisation.

Part IV

Implementation. Are you willing, ready and able?

Chapter 9

The implementation deception

While there are a host of clarification traps there is one big chasm into which decision makers fall on a regular basis. That is, the wonderful ability to deceive ourselves that our capability to implement is greater than it actually is. While your organisation may look and feel capable to you right now, how do you really know? More importantly, how do you know how it will fare when the going gets tough? Are you and your people ready, willing and able to see the job through, right to the end, no matter what it will take?

Understanding capability

Capability is such a misunderstood attribute in organisations. I feel we spend a lot of time working on organisational structures, management methods, the capability of individuals and productivity stimulants without truly understanding the intent of organisational design which is to deliver sufficient capability to meet our goals.

In a recent *Boss* magazine article, Andrew Thorburn, the CEO of National Australia Bank, one of Australia's largest banks, was talking about his focus as he tried to turn around the bank. He said, he wants management to focus on "people and capability, risk management and culture". I agree with Thorburn, however, I have a different spin on capability. My view of capability is that it needs to be viewed at the organisation level and not the person level. At the organisation level, culture and the ability to manage risk affect capability. While a builder wishes to hire a carpenter that can hammer nails, cut wood and assemble a structure, the builder also wants a carpenter that can manage uncertainty. In fact, the builder wants his organisation good at building and good at managing the uncertainty of building on time, to budget and to the functional requirements.

One of the earliest influencers of my thinking on organisational design is Herbert A. Simon through his ground-breaking book called *Administrative Behaviour*, first published in 1946. Simon describes the basis of an organisation as being a well-defined purpose communicated to staff and other stakeholders that leads to a series of decisions being taken that affect actions. The aim is to make the perfect decision to fulfil the organisational purpose and that means to understand all the possible flow-on consequences of a decision and choosing the right option. That is, of course, impossible. We can't predict the future with any degree of accuracy. Irrespective of the impossible nature of our task, we as leaders of organisations put into place policies, processes and systems to influence decision making and maximise the likelihood that the best decision to fulfil the organisational purpose is made. So an organisation is simply an assembly of people making decisions to act or not act. The quality of our decision making therefore defines our capability.

According to Simon, the great challenge leaders face is to manage the interpretation and errors in communication of policies, processes and systems. You know the old game where you all sit around in a circle and one person whispers an instruction to the person beside them and they then whisper it to the next person and so on until it gets back around to the first person. You then compare the initial instruction with the final version and you all laugh at how ridiculously different it is.

I have seen many corporate policies and frameworks in my time and to me it is obvious that the communication challenge starts with the design of policies and processes or systems. The one glaring tendency of policy designers is that they put too much information into policies, which puts those it's meant for off, or leaves them confused and in need of "training".

The other major communication challenge leaders have when it comes to influencing decisions was brought home to me when I was conducting a training program for middle managers. I ended with words to the effect that the challenge they had in their design of policies, processes and systems was to influence decision making so that people at the extremities of the organisation would make the same decision as the CEO would make. To my surprise this point was received with a great backlash. "Why do you assume the CEO will know what the right decision would be?" the participants said.

At that point it dawned on me that fulfilling organisational purpose is a two-way battle. The CEO and management are trying to influence downwards and staff are trying to influence upwards. Management think they know best and staff often think, "Management has no idea what the real issues are, sitting up there in their ivory tower!" Think of it as management has a magnetic rod pointed toward their north – "the big picture", while staff at the coal face have a magnetic rod pointed toward their north – "the customer". You end up with two like magnetic poles and you know what that means: the two poles repel each other. The flow of influencing is disrupted. So when you are designing your organisation's policies, processes and systems, you need to be thinking about how best to align the poles so the magnetic waves are working for you and not against you.

ALIGNING THE POLES

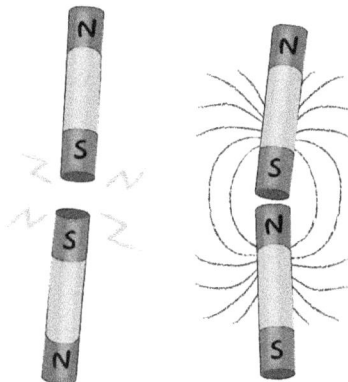

When the poles are aligned as they should be you have created the environment for optimal decision making and hence optimal capability.

Relentless execution

Someone who really understands the issue of capability is a military commander. In the Australian military they refer to capability managers, who in a Navy context would be the commander of a patrol boat or a frigate or the Admiral of a fleet of ships. The capability manager's role is to deliver the capability expected at the time it is asked. As an example, the capability manager for a fleet of frigates needs to be fully aware of the capability of each ship, the maintenance and supply providers, the current crew and any replacement crew. If the current mission is reliant on the army or air force, they need to know that they, too, are able to deliver. When it comes to the highest risk activities, there is no room for error as it would endanger lives.

It will come as no surprise then, that the CEO of Suncorp Group, Patrick Snowball, who is ex-British military, was successful in leading the insurance and banking group since he took over in a tough environment in 2009. Suncorp is capitalised at about $18 billion and the bulk of its revenues and profits come from insurance. It is also Australia's fifth largest bank.

What was the competitive landscape like in 2009? What challenges has Suncorp had to meet in the years that ensued and how has it fared for Snowball? To start with, the global financial crisis was in full swing and the bank's loan book was being hit.

In the main insurance business, insurance prices had peaked years before, around 2003, in the aftermath of the failure of Australian insurer HIH and the 9/11 terrorist event in New York, which stripped swathes of capital out of the insurance market. The Christchurch earthquakes and the Queensland cyclones and floods wreaked further havoc for insurers.

Being an Australian conglomerate it is usual to have close ties to New Zealand and so the earthquakes were a significant hit. Worse still, Suncorp's origins are in Queensland and the state is still its biggest market. The cyclones were its biggest exposure, however, cyclone exposure was well known and for the main it seems Suncorp was well reinsured so losses were contained.

What is perhaps of most interest is the Queensland floods. For the most part, flood insurance in Australia is hard to come by, at least at an affordable price. The problem is that most homes and businesses are not exposed to flooding. Those that are in flood zones are now well known to insurers so they either don't offer insurance cover or they charge according to the risk as they see it.

When the Brisbane floods occurred in 2011, it was not so much the claims that were a problem for the insurance industry, it was the potential damage to reputation as those who were affected by flood damage discovered they were either not insured or were not insured for enough. They had not read, or had not understood, their insurance policies.

During the previous years, Suncorp had decided to automatically cover flood. They invested in understanding flood risk through the use of flood maps. So, not only did they avoid the reputation damage, they were able to enhance their reputation. While Suncorp paid out significant sums in claims, they were very visible in ensuring the community knew they covered flood. The result was that many nervous buyers of insurance switched to Suncorp products.

Although some might argue that Snowball inherited a problem waiting to be fixed, you know and I know it is never as easy as that. Every basket case I ever took over got worse before I could make it better. The truth of the matter is that he had his challenges and he managed to provide a total shareholder return of 175 percent during his tenure. In comparison, rival Insurance Australia Group achieved 112 percent return in the same period.

On another measure, Snowball produced an 128 percent rise in share price compared with a 53 percent increase over the same period for Australia's top 200-listed companies as measured by the S&P/ASX200 index.[44]

Some of the key strategies Snowball has been praised for include the "one company, many brands" strategy, which tied different brands to shared values. Another was his so-called "building blocks" strategy, which addressed fundamental problems with the key processes and systems that were influencing decisions across the business.[45]

Snowball understood he had a capability problem at Suncorp.

44 Liew, Ruth (2015, April 17). "The snowball effect: Suncorp under departing CEO Patrick Snowball." *The Sydney Morning Herald*
45 ibid

He ensured strategies to address them were designed, and most importantly he made sure his team saw them through. You will not be surprised to hear that one of his favourite mottoes was "relentless execution". Being ex-military, Snowball, now retired, was fully aware of the need for meticulous planning and that every plan needed a contingency as there are no guarantees of success. Relentless execution means both executing the plan and modifying the plan as circumstances change to ensure desired outcomes are achieved.

Choose to be agile

How ready to relentlessly execute should you be? A good question. It comes back to: What is the purpose you are trying to fulfil? At the opposite extremes of purpose, driven by survival at one end and values at the other, the more relentless you will want to be. If you are following desire, the more you thirst for your goal, the more you will want to be relentless.

As you make progress towards fulfilling your purpose, you will also need to start thinking about protecting what you have created. You will need to start thinking of how you will enshrine the inherent value you have created. It is so easy to lose what you have gained.

What does it take to enshrine value? The first rule is never bet more than you can afford to lose. That is, as you take on challenges, and take on risk, you will need to keep something in reserve. If you bet too much and lose you are out of the game. Your ability to pursue your purpose has been lost.

The essence of this age-old advice was captured by Nassim Taleb who I referred to earlier. In his book *The Black Swan, The Impact of the Highly Improbable*, he makes a good argument that some things are simply impossible to predict (remember the story of the Black Swan) and that you should always keep something in reserve.[46] Taleb also devised a most interesting investment strategy that is drawn from the same realisation that some things simply can't be predicted. His strategy is to keep 95 percent of investments in low-risk, safe havens and to risk the living daylights out of the other 5 percent on highly speculative investments like movies, mining exploration companies and pharmaceutical companies with big research and development budgets. The crux of it is there are highly improbable upsides just as there are highly improbable downsides and you need to be prepared for both. If you are not in the game you cannot hope to take advantage of the upsides and if you lose too much you have to leave the game.

Enshrining value is one part of being prepared for relentless execution. However, the key to it is agility. What is the biggest difference between small and large organisations? Agility. How often do large organisations underestimate how long it will take to execute a strategy? Answer, almost all of the time.

What does agility look like? To answer that question I will bring you back to what an organisation is. A bunch of

---

46 Taleb, Nassim (2007). *The Black Swan: The Impact of the Highly Improbable*, Random House, N.Y.

people making decisions. So in order to be agile we need agile decision making. We need to ensure people are informed, that there is an agreed process to make a decision and that the decision is adequately communicated. Think how that flows right through to when the greatest agility is needed: when we experience crisis.

When a crisis hits, if we are not prepared and we don't know where to get the information we need, we can't agree on who has the authority to decide and we can't communicate the information to the people that need to know; we are like deer caught in the headlights. We are stunned and stuck and the world passes us by. There is no better example of how important these concepts are than the story of Nokia versus Ericsson when a key supplier to both of them had a mishap in the year 2000.

The supplier was Philips and they manufactured radio frequency chips for cell phones at their Albuquerque, New Mexico facility in the US. They had a small fire that was managed onsite. A few racks of chips were burnt. However, chips are seriously fragile and the resulting smoke and water damage from the fire and the fire fighting was much more widespread. It turned out millions of chips were damaged, setting back supply and production of millions of mobile phones.[47]

Across the North Atlantic at the Nokia plant near Helsinki, Finland, a planner noticed something was amiss because he did

---

47 Mukherjee, Amit S (2009). *The Spider's Strategy : Creating Networks to Avert Crisis, Create Change and Really Get Ahead*, FT Press, Upper Saddle River, N.J.

not receive some information from the supplier on time as he was expecting. He escalated it as an event and so a potential chip supply issue was on a few people's radars. When Philips worked out the severity of their problem they got in touch with both Ericsson and Nokia a few days later. Nokia immediately initiated increased tracking of the problem and assumed Philips would take longer than they indicated to recover. As their assumptions proved true they moved to their contingency plans and sought other suppliers and modified designs to allow alternate supply. Ericsson did little. They didn't have the systems in place to provide early warning of the problem, or to fully appreciate the scale of the potential problem. Nokia did the hard-smart work, Ericsson didn't. The end result, Nokia reported a 42 percent profit rise for the quarter and Ericsson reported a loss in that quarter and further quarters.[48]

It's a choice to be sufficiently agile to enshrine hard-earned positions in markets, or in the case of not-for-profits in the minds of the public and of governments. As you well know, the bigger you are, the more ingrained is the bureaucracy, and the harder it is to choose and deliver agility.

Preparation is key

Almost anything is possible if you have the capability and the right decision-making processes to ensure you are fully prepared. I am sure of this because I had the pleasure of hearing Alisa

---

48 Ibid

Camplin tell her story at a Thought Leaders Business School keynote presentation.[49]

Camplin won a gold medal in aerial skiing at the 2002 Salt Lake City Winter Olympics. She started her story by describing her determination as a young athlete. She described how she was super competitive and how she developed an incredibly powerful dream to one day make the Olympics and to win gold for Australia. The problem was, while she was good, in fact very good, so were her competitors. While she shined for her home state of Victoria, she was not quite good enough to make international competitions. Camplin moved from athletics, to gymnastics, to field hockey to sailing. In all these sports she won state or national medals.

One day, while pondering what more she could do to make her gold medal dream come true, Camplin came up with the idea of finding a new sport. One that she may have the physical skills for, one to which she could apply her determination to succeed and perhaps, just maybe, she could fulfil her dream. She looked at all the different sports, what types of physical skills were required and the mental fortitude that would be needed. She landed on aerial skiing.

You might find it surprising that Camplin chose aerial skiing, given that she was now 19 and didn't know how to ski. In fact, she had never even seen snow. While this would seem

---

49 Camplin, Alisa, (2014, November 27). Keynote Address, Thought Leaders Business School, Melbourne.

an insurmountable problem for most of us, Camplin saw it differently. She saw that a country like Australia, so far behind the Winter Olympic powerhouse countries of Europe and North America, could provide the support to someone like compatriot Kirstie Marshall who had won World Cup gold medals and competed and placed competitively at the 1994 and 1998 Winter Olympics. Camplin had the right physique and the gymnastic athleticism and she knew she had the mental fortitude to train, train and train. To complete the "10,000 hours to become an expert" which Malcolm Gladwell writes about in *Outliers.*[50] All she needed to do was to get the right training.

Camplin picked up the phone and called the Australian Institute of Sport and asked to speak to Marshall's coach. After handling a few difficult questions she managed to get through to Marshall's manager and to convince him to meet with her. When they met she asked what it would take to be the best in the world in aerial skiing. What was needed to win a gold medal? Besides being able to ski, the manager rattled off a list of key attributes including financial and emotional support. She mapped the mastery of these attributes to her end goal of making the Olympic team and competing for gold and gave herself eight years to do so, the time lapse until the 2002 Winter Olympics. She confirmed with the manager the goals she would need to achieve within the first year in order to achieve her eight-year goal. At the end of the meeting, the manager agreed

---

50 Gladwell, Malcolm (2008). *Outliers*, Allen Lane. Camberwell, Vic.

that if she achieved the goals set for year one that he would become her mentor.

Yes, Camplin did achieve her year-one goals and her eight-year journey could continue. Her story is remarkable to say the least. Her list of injuries over the following years including brutal bone, knee and shoulder injuries along with multiple concussions; all the evidence I needed to know she was determined. However, we all know determination is not all that is required. What was even more impressive was the extent of her preparation.

Camplin took the Boy Scout motto, "be prepared", to an extreme I had not heard of before outside of the military or the world of the astronaut. The reason it seems was in large part due to her day job.

While on her gold-medal quest Camplin was an IBM employee. She later became a successful manager. However, while not too far into her quest she was attending a meeting which included a presentation by one of IBM's leading sales professionals. They had a very important contract they wanted to keep and all the best minds across the business and the best business tools were being brought to the table. The tool that caught Camplin's attention was a risk matrix. The sales professional was using it to describe the varying level of importance of the various risks the team had identified that would need to be managed to achieve the goal of re-winning the contract. From that day on, Camplin actively used the risk management process to fulfil her personal goal.

My favourite story of Camplin's, is about the one and only photograph she has displayed in her home of herself competing as an aerial skier. It is a photo of her at a World Cup event and in it she is standing at the top of her run, poised to start the jump. Standing behind her is her coach, holding an umbrella above her. Camplin explained that in between jumps there is plenty of standing around on the slopes and that every now and then the conditions turn to rain rather than snow and you get wet and horribly cold. On the day the photo was taken, she was the only competitor on the hill that had planned sufficiently ahead, for all conditions, and had packed an umbrella!

What else did Camplin say that she had done to prepare, and to manage the uncertainties that she might confront? She did things like stay up all night and then train so she knew what it felt like to be running on adrenalin with little sleep when competing. The risk she was concerned about was that she might be too excited or nervous to sleep well the night before the gold-medal competition. She also prepared contingency plans for things like extended weather delays. What would she do, where and how, she asked herself. She planned and planned.

Camplin brings together all of the key attributes to manage the implementation deception. She knew her capability and she knew that that alone was not enough to guarantee success. She knew she would have to be super prepared to be in the best possible position to execute flawlessly. Camplin realised her dream and won gold at the 2002 Winter Olympics, Salt Lake City, US. It was the second gold ever for Australia at a Winter Olympics.

Will you know?

Another element of the implementation deception is not thinking through how you are going to monitor the implementation of your decision so you can manage the uncertainties you may have identified and detect the ones you overlooked. We don't do enough thinking about monitoring key indicators, and we certainly don't do enough about monitoring capability.

Take capability for starters. How do you currently measure the capability of your organisation? If you are like most organisations you do some or all of the following: you monitor financials on a monthly basis; you run an engagement survey of employees because it is well recognised as a key ingredient for performance; you also have an employee-performance-management program, where at least once a year, your employees sit with their manager to review their performance, to set new goals and to identify development needs; you have risk profiles to alert management to the level of risk posed to planned objectives; you also have informal ways of monitoring capability; and, you have meetings to discuss customer issues and other challenges in the business.

What is wrong with this picture? It is piecemeal. You don't have a clear methodology of understanding your organisation's capability. Capability is made up of many aspects from how much money you have in your war chest, to the skills and knowledge of your people, to how well the organisation is set up to succeed. This can include the infrastructure that has been invested in it and how you have structured the organisation. And of course, culture is a big part of capability. Are our people engaged? Are they working collaboratively? Are they motivated in the right way to avoid poor decision making to achieve their own bonuses? While attempts have been made at building organisational performance monitoring that you could construe as having been designed to deliver a clearer picture of organisational capability, such as the balanced scorecard approach, in truth, corporate performance-management systems are generally assessments of an organisation's progress towards set goals. Where performance is noted as being off-track, interventions are required. The questions you should be asking are: Why was it off-track? and, how could I have avoided it?

In a perfect world you would have a complete understanding of your organisation's capability and you would drive your organisation to extend itself right to the limit of that capability. Instead, we assume a level of a capability and we monitor mostly lag indicators of performance to find out how wrong we were. You would be much better developing a clear methodology of assessing your organisation's capability and monitoring it as frequently as necessary.

How often are you monitoring your financial outcomes? Monthly, right? How often are you reporting against your business plan? Perhaps quarterly or six-monthly? How often are you monitoring your people? Perhaps six-monthly? Perhaps you run an annual culture survey? Why are you measuring financials monthly, but only monitoring your people every six months on some measures and annually, at best, on others? And don't forget, you are not even measuring actual capability of the organisation as a package.

Wouldn't it be smarter to monitor capability as a package much more often, at least quarterly, and make adjustments long before your lag performance indicators go off the rails? Think of a trucking company. What would be key to measuring performance? Number one, as with most for-profit businesses, would be gross-profit margin. The difference between the cost of delivery versus the price it is delivered at. What else? Monitoring the oil price would be sensible. That would indicate if our margins are being squeezed by increasing fuel costs. Both are indicators of performance and impact on performance. What else could we measure? If our employees are engaged, if our maintenance people are keeping up with the latest in truck maintenance, if our truck drivers are following the law and taking the breaks they should, and if they are driving their vehicles economically, measured by distance travelled for the volume of fuel consumed.

What is missing? An assessment of capability. An assessment of our overall capability to manage a rise in fuel costs, to ensure our maintenance performance continues to be of a high standard, to ensure we hire, train and nurture the right truck drivers? Take the Australian Department of Defence. They have capability as a fundamental goal for the organisation and they have the concept of FICs, or fundamental inputs to capability. They are asking, do we have the right personnel, organisation (organisational design), major systems (plant and equipment), supplies, facilities and training areas, support and command and management to allow the organisation to deliver military capability as and when needed? They have developed a military model of capability. In my experience, very few organisations have developed a capability model for their organisation, a model which would allow them to identify gaps and monitor those gaps to drive improvement.

I explained this to one of my clients without thinking that they would take it on board without any further consultation with me. What was the result? They tasked human resources with assessing capability. What did HR do? They interviewed a swathe of management and staff. What did they find? A raft of problems, which was not a surprise to anyone as their performance had been suffering for some time. The problem was they did not start with a methodology for assessing capability, which would have given them the ability to map capability across the organisation and compare different areas of the business. This is important to identify both where they needed to intervene most urgently and where there were common ailments that required a cross-divisional approach. They simply ended up with a list of headaches and no idea of where to start to apply remedies. The result was an even more deflated management team with a greater feeling of being overwhelmed with problems they had created for themselves.

If you do not have a sound method for understanding and monitoring capability you shouldn't be surprised to find that the implementation deception has and will continue to be one of the biggest pitfalls in your decision making and the decision making of others in your organisation. Thinking of the adage, measure what matters, when it comes to making decisions, nothing matters more than understanding your own capability.

Once you have an understanding of your capability to deliver on a goal, you also need to find a few other key measures that are strong lead indicators of future success. Much has been said recently about big data and the gold that is buried within. While this may be true in some instances, what is more likely happening in your world is that because of big data, because of the power of computing, because of the hype, you and the people around you are being pressured into measuring just about anything that is not nailed to the floor. What do you end up with? Too many people, spending too much time producing too many KPIs that do not result in more effective decision making. Have you ever considered the cost of all that measurement? One of my clients with around 20,000 employees estimated the cost of collating the data to track their 5,000 plus list of key performance goals was well into the millions of dollars!

Here is an anecdote from the global financial crisis. The finance sector in the first half of the first decade of this century was busy analysing markets, building sophisticated risk models to measure the key indicators of the market and making billions of dollars. Then the sub-prime mortgage market disintegrated as interest rates went up and the whole system imploded with the tipping point being the collapse of Lehman Bros. Why did this happen? First the risk managers and their faulty models were blamed. Eventually it all came out that the greed mindset of Wall Street and elsewhere around the world had created blocks to sound decision making. The leaders of financial organisations had become blinded to the realities.

I remember after the 1987 stock market crash when an investment industry pundit being interviewed said, "You know it's time to get out of the market when your taxi driver is discussing stock market picks!" The period 2006 to 2008 had the same feel about it. Many people I knew, including myself, called it a bubble. Of course the art was to pick the moment before the bubble burst. While I called the 2008 bust two years early, I did not suffer like those who exchanged stock picks with their taxi driver right up to the proverbial pin prick that was Lehman Bros.

What happened next was inevitable. A call for more regulation and boy, did the banking sector cop it. In July 2014, the CFO of Citibank announced that by year-end they would have nearly 30,000 staff globally working on regulatory and compliance issues.[51] That represented a one-third increase in staff in these areas since 2011. At the same time, JP Morgan Chase reported they would spend an additional US$4 billion on risk-control staff.[52]

Through all the modelling and through all the measurement leading up to the global financial crisis, or GFC, the key players

---

51 From: http://blogs.marketwatch.com/thetell/2014/07/14/citi-will-have-almost-30000-employees-in-compliance-by-year-end/

52 From: http://blogs.marketwatch.com/thetell/2014/07/14/citi-will-have-almost-30000-employees-in-compliance-by-year-end/

in the banking industry had not been measuring what really mattered. What really mattered was greed and factoring greed into a risk model. Greed may have been difficult to measure, however, the fact that it was missing from all measurement models highlights the "Will you know?" part of the implementation deception. When deciding to go into sub-prime markets, what the banks needed to think about was, "How are we going to know when our assumptions that go into our models are no longer valid?" If they decided they could not know that, then a different approach should have been taken to the market. Alternatively, if they could answer that question effectively then they were in a position to take advantage of the upside and get out before the inevitable happened: the bursting of the bubble.

Measuring and reporting on scores of KPIs doesn't lead to more effective decision making. It gobbles up valuable time of your best and brightest to produce the information and to read it to find what is truly important. What you need to do is measure what matters and what truly matters is the core information that will determine if you change your course of action. That is, the information on which you will decide to act or not act.

Beware milestones

Having convinced you to improve your measurement of what really matters in your organisation so that you can make better decisions, I must provide a word of caution. Sometimes when we introduce new measures we actually hurt decision making. Take the effect that milestones have on people.

Milestones as the name infers are solid markers of progress on a journey. You have either made the milestone or you have fallen short. There is no better example of the effect of milestones on decision making than from sport.

Take the game of cricket. If you don't know cricket all you need to focus in on is one number, 100. That number represents a century of runs by a batsman in one innings and is a massive milestone. Careers are judged on the number of centuries a batsman scores.

A batsman plays the game to score runs by hitting a ball sent toward him at varying speeds of up to 100.2 miles per hour (161.3 kilometres per hour) by a bowler from 22 yards (20 metres) away. The 100.2 mph delivery, officially the fastest ball ever recorded, was delivered by Shoaib Akhtar of Pakistan. Shoaib was nicknamed the Rawalpindi Express!

Needless to say, scoring runs is not dead easy. A great batting average in cricket at the highest levels is 40 plus and you are among the elite when you have an average over 50. Then there is Australia's great Don Bradman who had an average of 99.94 with his next nearest rivals being South Africa's Graeme Pollock with 60.97 and England's Herb Sutcliffe with 60.63. Bradman was truly a master batsman.

At the other end of the spectrum are the non-specialist batsmen, the bowlers that are required to bat, just like pitchers in the National League in US baseball, except you can't substitute them out for a good batsmen just when you need one. The batting average for your typical number 11 batsmen is less than 10 runs.

Now take yourself to the 2013 Ashes Tour of England by the Australian cricket team. Enter one Ashton Agar, a 19-year-old bowler who could "bat a bit". He makes his debut for Australia against England in the first test match of a five-test series. Agar is slotted in the number-11 batting position. England don't perform well in their first innings (of two) and the Australian team members are feeling pretty good about themselves. Then disaster strikes, Australia loses nine of 10 wickets and they have barely made half the runs England made. Agar walks onto the field and starts scoring runs immediately and almost at will. Together with regular batsman, the late Phil Hughes, they build a partnership that takes the score well past England's score. Before you knew it, with the greatest of ease, Ashton was approaching the milestone all cricketers strive for, to score a century, 100 runs in one innings.

What happened next was the strongest evidence you will ever need of the dangers of milestones. Agar had already achieved massive success. He had already scored more runs by a number-11 batsman than ever before in over 120 years of test cricket. He and Phil Hughes now had the highest partnership for the last wicket of an innings. Agar had helped save his team in the all-important first test. However, he could see that milestone looming, a century. Not just any century, a century on debut, an even more significant milestone, and a century by a number-11 batsman!

People who follow cricket are well aware of the saying "the nervous nineties". It was palpable. The free scoring Agar tensed up. He scored one run in the 62nd over, one in the 63rd and edged nervously for three runs in the 64th, he was then four runs from glory. On the second ball of the 65th over he defended again for a comfortable two runs. He was just two runs away from glory. Here is how the ESPN Cricinfo website commentator called it for online followers:[53]

> 64.3
>
> Broad to Agar, no run, back of a length down the leg side, swings at it and misses
>
> 64.4
>
> Broad to Agar, no run, short again, wafts at it trying to force it down to third man past gully but missed
>
> 64.5
>
> Broad to Agar, OUT, back of a length, pulled and ... got him! Oh no, caught in the deep. A miscue aiming to the midwicket boundary but didn't get it and Graeme Swann came in and took a low catch. He came so close, having played so well, but Agar has fallen just short of an historical century but it's still the highest test score by a no. 11

For those watching live as I was, you could see how his behaviour had changed. He, the commentators and I were all left at best flat, and at worst distraught.

You may be thinking, he was young and inexperienced, of course he became anxious. If he was a 10-year veteran he would have been okay. Well I have two examples to dispel that truth.

---

53 From: http://www.espncricinfo.com/the-ashes-2013/engine/match/566932.
html?innings=1;view=commentary

One is the great Indian cricket batsman Sachin Tendulkar. In fact, many would say he was the greatest, even better than Don Bradman. Although Tendulkar never reached a batting average anywhere near Bradman's he did have other amazing achievements. After 52 tests, the same number as Bradman played in his career, which was interrupted by World War II, Tendulkar was averaging 49.77 runs compared with Bradman's 99.94. Tendulkar reached a career-high of 58.46 after 103 tests. While the numbers show a big gap between the two players, Tendulkar played in a different era, an era that included one-day international (ODI) cricket. His career consisted of 200 test matches and 463 one-day internationals and ran from November 1989 until November 2013, some 24 years. A truly remarkable career. Most remarkably, he scored 100 centuries across the two forms of the game. He scored 51 test hundreds and 49 ODI hundreds. So how can a man with so much experience, with so much already achieved, feel milestone pressure?

In January 2011, Tendulkar scored the last of his 51 test centuries to leave him on 97 hundreds across both forms of the game. By mid-March he had scored two more ODI centuries. With the pressure of the milestone and the fear his skills were waning ever so slightly as each month passed, it took the great man another year and 13 attempts before he finally made a century of centuries on March 16, 2012.

Another example to show that age and experience are not the big determinants of those who feel the pressure of a milestone and those who do not, is from the career of the great US golfer Tom

Watson. This example highlights that a key determinant is how important the milestone is to a person. Watson first played on the PGA Tour in 1968. His last full year on tour was in 1999, although he has played in PGA events every year since. He has had 39 tour wins, including eight major championship wins between 1975 and 1983.He is ranked sixth on the PGA all-time list of major champions.

At the 2009 British Open at Turnberry in Scotland, at the age of 59, Watson was teed up to compete to win his ninth major and the Claret Jug for the sixth time. He knew the course, he had won the championship there in 1977. Surely he didn't have high expectations. After the first round he was tied second, after the second round he was tied first, after the third round he was the leader by one shot. I can't capture the drama of the finishing holes in words here, you will have to go online for that.[54] It was captivating. Watson had about a nine-foot putt on the 18th to win. All I can say is that he probably didn't hit a worse putt on any of the preceding 71 holes played over four days. If you have played the game seriously you will know what pressure can do to your golf swing and your putting stroke. The pressure of hitting the milestone, of becoming the oldest winner ever of a major was too much, even for an experienced veteran. He went on to lose to Stewart Cink in a four-hole play-off by six shots!

Even worse, you may find you have a Nick Leeson on your hands. Leeson was a rogue trader who reportedly single-

---

54 See: https://www.youtube.com/watch?v=_0ao-M3wx8Y

handedly brought down Barings Bank in 1995. Barings was the UK's oldest investment bank dating back to the 18th century. Remember, not every fraudster has to be a financial trader. They just need intent and they will find a way to make the numbers to earn the recognition they are seeking. It is not always money. It can be kudos, for example. Think of academic Rusi Taleyarkhan who claimed to have effectively created tabletop nuclear fusion, which implied a potentially boundless source of cheap energy. In 2008, he was found guilty of misconduct by a committee established by his employers, Purdue University, for deliberately misleading others about the research.

The next time you are thinking about setting targets, think how an employee will feel when they reach 98 out of 100 for a bonus target. Score 100, they get a bonus. Score 98, they get nothing, zip. Think of the decisions you are tempting some people to make. People start thinking, how can I game the system to score the extra two points I need? They may drop the margin in a proposal or a sales offer to get the sale before the bonus KPI cut-off date. Had they not had the pressure, they may well have cut a better deal a week or two later.

Beware of milestones because of the change in behaviour they may create in some people – people who have drivers that create blockers to sound decision making. Drivers like greed and ego, or the desire to be seen as the best or simply just better.

Chapter 10

You create your destiny

When it comes to our bigger, strategic decisions, overconfidence in our capability is the single biggest implementation deception. Therefore it is by default the single greatest opportunity. In his book *Left Brain, Right Stuff: How Leaders Make Winning Decisions*, Phil Rosenzweig argues that overconfidence is a misused term when it comes to decision making. He asks, "overconfidence with respect to what?" As he points out, having self-belief is extremely important to overachieve, to outperform. Without confidence, and more than the average amount of it, you are unlikely to win the close matches, whether they be in sport or business. Rosenzweig calls it having "the right stuff". That is, in his studies of decision making, the leaders that had "the right stuff" took on challenges that others wouldn't and won.

I feel Rosenzweig is right in many ways, however, it might be a case of which came first, the chicken or the egg. In my experience, the leaders I have met that have "the right stuff" are also the people that are not afraid to do the hard-smart work. They will do what it takes to clarify what they are getting themselves into and what skills and experience they can bring to meet the challenge at hand. As importantly, when they decide to act, they systematically create their own destiny by assembling and building a team that will deliver the job. So when Rosenzweig talks of leaders with the "right stuff" he is not talking about those with bravado only, he is talking about those with bravado who are also smart.

How does a smart leader create their destiny? Essentially they build their success. First they define the purpose of the organisation or team and put the strategy they are embarking on into context. They clearly define the outcomes that will fulfil the purpose. They then choose leaders, who form teams of talented people. Together they set about creating the right environment for their people, providing them direction and giving them focus. Finally they monitor performance. When they see the laying of a strong foundation they build on it. When they see fault with the foundation, they fix it and rework it to be sure it is a solid base on which to grow. As the structure starts to form they look for ways to build faster, more efficiently and at less cost. More importantly they look to innovate. How can we improve the original design? When one team makes an improvement, the other teams are encouraged to build off it. Before long, one success leads to another and the smart leader is in that wonderful position where success cascades.

Of course, cascading success requires plenty to go right and not so much to go wrong. So let's have a look at each stage of the process so you can implement your strategic decisions faster and more smoothly than ever before. Start with purpose.

The power of purpose

From early on in this book I have spoken about purpose. How it is a strong motivator, how if people are not clear on purpose or are not fully aligned they may not make the best decisions. In finding your creators of your success, the ones that are going to give you your cascading successes, you will need to harness the "power of purpose".

President Kennedy's mission of "landing a man on the moon and returning him safely to the Earth" caused the creation of leaders, teams and many remarkable individuals that worked together to create the destiny JFK had mapped out. Kennedy gave the people of the US, in particular those in NASA, a true vision of the future. He gave them a powerful purpose. The extent of the power of that purpose is brought home to us by the story of JFK and the NASA janitor. The story goes that JFK was visiting NASA in 1962 and he approached a janitor who was carrying a broom and asked what the man was doing. The man replied, "Well, Mr President I'm helping put a man on the moon."[55]

---

55 Nemo, John (2014, Dec. 23). "What a NASA janitor can teach us about living a bigger life." *Denver Business Journal.*

Put simply, purpose inspires us. It motivates us to overcome obstacles, to work together to fulfil a common goal. Below are some examples of how organisations articulate their purpose in the hope of inspiring others:

- Walmart – "To help people save money so they can live better."
- General Electric – "We bring good things to life."
- Daimler – "To produce cars and trucks that people will want to buy, will enjoy driving and will want to buy again."
- Citigroup – "To improve the quality of life for children, families and the neighbourhood where we all live and do business."
- Samsung – "To lead the digital convergence movement."
- Nestle – "Make better food so that people lead a better life."
- Honda – "To seek technology that helps realise true peace and happiness on earth."
- Fiat – "To create mobility that has a truly human dimension."
- United Health Group – "To help people lead healthier lives."

And then there is Apple. According to *The Economist*, Steve Jobs's mission statement for Apple in 1980 was, "To make a contribution to the world by making tools for the mind that advance humankind."[56]

---

56 "Mission statement,"*The Economist*. Retrieved from: http://www.economist.com/node/13766375

Now a word of caution. Purpose is powerful and in the words of Superman's father, "Use your powers for good instead of evil." Not everyone has Superman's father to advise them and sometimes purpose can lead to ruin. I am not talking about the obvious baddies, the hardened criminals or terrorists. I am talking about ordinary people caught up in a maelstrom of hype and activity towards a goal that, if they had had the chance to stop and look at what they were doing from a distance, they would see it wasn't acceptable to the common man or woman.

There are the obvious ones like the protagonist in the movie *The Wolf of Wall Street*, Enron, or the big investment banks and their selling of collateralised debt obligations, which contributed to the 2008 economic crisis and the collapse of Lehman Brothers. There is also the controversy around high frequency trading started by Michael Lewis, and described in his book *Flash Boys*. Lewis' book is an exposé of how firms can position themselves, geographically, closer to the exchanges to take advantage of the milliseconds it takes for a trade to be transacted in the market. One company built a direct-fibre-optic link between the New York and Chicago exchanges. High-frequency traders can note a large transaction and buy or sell the stock in front of it, to take advantage of the price movement that comes with the large trade. It is a controversial exposé because the large banks, the stock exchanges and even the US government refute the claims made in the book. However, as reported in *USA Today* in May, 2014, the US Securities and Exchange Commission fined the New York Stock Exchange $4.5 million for providing "co-location" services which allowed traders to place their laptops closer to the servers transacting the business.[57] Perhaps we have not seen the end of that story.

The purpose of making money is one powerful driver that causes people to make less than optimum decisions. What are the others? Fame? Yes, look at all the athletes that use drugs to win. That feeling you get when you are standing on top of the podium is a powerful driver.

Not just athletes seek fame. Many business people want to leave their mark, to be "known for something", something big. Driving the organisation hard towards a goal, which will see them lauded if it comes off can lead to ruin. However, being bold, like JFK was with the Apollo mission, can result in great leaders leaving an indelible mark. But, you need to strike a balance.

The last example of purpose gone wrong that I would like to point out to you is a sad one. It involves those institutions that for the most part are trying to do good in the world, however, because they become blinded by their purpose there is collateral damage along the way. The not-for-profit organisations that caused the greatest harm in the 20th century in first-world countries are the institutions to whom children were entrusted. Religious, education and cultural institutions

---

57 Krantz, Matt, (2014, May 1). "USA Today, Rigged market? SEC busts the NYSE". *USA Today Money*.

all failed us. In Australia, the harm caused resulted in the formation of a Royal Commission into Institutional Responses to Child Sex Abuse. The second volume of the commission's interim report has 150 personal accounts, a mere selection, of horrific treatment by those in authority in organisations established for a "good purpose". Organisations that didn't respond appropriately when they became aware of the abuse of children because they didn't want the reputational damage that would impact on the fulfilment of their purpose.

Beware of the potential power of your purpose and channel it "for good instead of evil". Create your "super-people" to become your creators, however, coach and guide them as their cascading success could blind them from some harsh realities.

Creative leaders

With your purpose and its potential power clarified in your mind, it's time to take a look at your leadership team. Is it the right team for the job? Do they have, or does the team collectively have, "the right stuff"?

What I look for in a team leader is creativity. I look for a person that is not afraid to experiment, is willing to learn and when they see the opportunity they grasp it and turn it into true innovation. Great team leaders also have the ability to build trust, to be decisive when needed and consultative when not and to be calm and be able to hold a room when the moment calls for it. Couple these traits with a willingness to experiment, learn and innovate and you have yourself a creator that will help build the cascading success your strategic decision requires to ensure it is a successful one.

Why is experimentation so important for a leader? Experimentation is the domain of scientists and they have a highly considered approach to establishing facts. First they establish theories and then try to disprove them. They design a multitude of experiments that should, if successful, disprove the theory. If they can't disprove it they become increasingly comfortable with the theory as a fact, without ever being able to prove their theory 100 percent. Similarly in business, we can never guarantee the success of a new product, but we can certainly increase our knowledge and hence our comfort levels by challenging the original theory with a few well-designed experiments.

How valuable is a creative leader? One who experiments and finds their way through difficult channels? Look no further than the valuation of tech companies like Facebook.

On May 18, 2012, Facebook listed on the US NASDAQ exchange with a valuation in the vicinity of a US$100 billion on annualised earnings of only US$500 million. Almost two years later on February 19, 2014, the market capitalisation was about US$170 billion, while the social networking company's 2013 earnings were around US$2 billion. This made for a price-earnings ratio, or PE, of more than 100; more than five times the PE of US industrial stocks. The inflated PE of Facebook reflects the value placed on the creative ability, the intellectual capital, of Facebook. Investors believed that the creativity of leaders of Facebook would be able to achieve much larger earnings in the future.

When you think about the future of thought processing and decision making across all sectors of our society, the more relevance creative leadership must have. We have long known that the amount of data is growing exponentially. Wiki's, on Wikidpedia, have moved from terabytes to petabytes, exabytes, zettabytes and now yottabytes, which is 10 to the power of 8 kilobytes. However data alone does not create knowledge, it simply creates opportunity to enhance knowledge. Creative leaders will be the ones who can devise the experiments that will turn data into knowledge, a step away from competitive advantage. All that is needed is that bit of spark to ignite a successful execution.

Looking for a practical example? Look no further than Ron Kohavi, Microsoft Distinguished Engineer and General Manager of the Analysis and Experimentation team at Microsoft's Applications and Services Group. Prior to joining Microsoft he was director of data mining and personalisation at Amazon.com, where he found many examples of how experimentation can bring great rewards.

In a presentation entitled "Practical Guide to Controlled Experiments on the Web: Listen to Your Customers not to the HiPPO", Kohavi describes a simple experiment run by Greg Linden of Amazon. Linden had the idea that as people added items to their shopping carts they would have other items recommended to them based on the items they had placed into the cart. You may now be familiar with the offer, "other people who bought this item also bought ..."

The experiment Linden proposed was to establish whether showing the recommendation would cross-sell more items and increase the average sale size or if it would distract people from checking out, make it all too hard for them and would result in a loss of sales. Enter what Kohavi refers to as the "HiPPO (Highest Paid Person's Opinion)" who had recommended to stop the project all together. Despite the HIPPO, Linden was allowed to run the experiment anyway. It was hugely successful and the rest is history.

Kohavi with his teams at Microsoft have explored the value of experimentation over many years and he has come to the conclusion that people think too short-term, that they are fearful that an experiment will fail and consequently there is a cultural resistance to experimentation. Kohavi has also worked out that, "Our intuition is poor, especially on novel ideas." Enough said, creative leadership is where it is at.

Now this might be stating the obvious, however, there are creative types and then there are creative types. As one of my colleagues from Thought Leaders Global, Oscar Trimboli, once wrote: "Great musicians can explore creativity when they have practiced the basics relentlessly." So wind your mind back to the section on relentless execution in Chapter 9 and be sure you are choosing your leaders on that basis first, with all the other fine traits you are looking for. Then look for the gold, their creative ability.

Talented teams

To ensure the cascading success you are looking for, you will need to support your creative leaders in building talented teams. Talented teams are those with the right mix of skills and attitudes for the challenge ahead. Skills are, of course, dependent on the challenge, while attitudes relate directly to the extent of alignment of the individual to the purpose of the team and the organisation. Once you have a team with the right skills and attitudes, their job is simply to identify the gaps between what they have achieved and what they need to achieve, to build bridges and to get the traffic moving across them. The traffic could be data, it could be customers, it could be money. Whatever it is, it needs to flow across bridges built for the purpose. Not too expensive yet solid. Taking account of aesthetics as much as possible, yet not being distracted by the need for it to look unique. And the bridges must be built to transverse the real gaps and must be built in the right priority order. Many decisions need to be made.

Now is the time to remember the value of a decision. The value of the strategic decision that you made and which has led to the creation of the teams of talented people you will need is, of course, the most valuable based on a volume measure. However, as I pointed out earlier, following every great decision there are literally thousands, or even tens of thousands, of decisions that follow that will make or break the original decision. While individuals make decisions all the time, when they are part of a team the lasting decision is usually made by the team, led by the team leader. It is in the decision making of your talented teams that the rubber hits the road. Your job is to ensure, as far as is reasonably practical, that the right decision is made in pursuit of the organisational purpose.

The normal and required response of organisations is to respond with policies, processes and systems. The secret of course is to have the right blend of directed work and self-directed work. Contrast the different experiences of two of my friends who have changed jobs recently. One left IBM and joined CSC and the other left SAP and joined IBM. These are all large global tech companies. IBM has more than 400,000 employees, while CSC and SAP both have more than 70,000.

The one who left IBM after a long and successful career worked mostly from home and spoke of the mostly clear and well-thought out policies and processes within which he operated. When he moved to CSC he had to negotiate working from home two days a week as it was not the cultural norm. Nor were CSC's policies and processes like what he had experienced at IBM.

On the other hand, my friend who left SAP commented after just a few weeks at IBM how obsessed the organisation was with process. At SAP, the focus had been on getting the organisation a return on their investment in him, that is getting him productive; at IBM it was all about ensuring he followed their processes of induction and learning.

Now one might think that because IBM has more than 400,000 employees and the others had sub 100,000 that perhaps size is what mattered. My friend and I agreed that once you get into the tens of thousands, it isn't a case for a need for an increased ratio of processes to staff to manage them. For IBM it was simply how they do business. Same for SAP's and CSC's approaches.

I didn't take the opportunity to explore in any scientific way the relationship between the extent of processes and the extent staff were operating under directed and self-directed work. One could observe, however, given all of these organisations are successful in their own right that it is not the number of policies, processes and systems that matter, it is how they guide decision making of staff and, in particular, team leaders. It is the extent to which staff feel they have guidance, and also autonomy. That guidance may be found within a policy or process on the company intranet, or it can be found from a colleague a few desks away.

This challenge of balancing the extent of directed and self-directed work has never been more evident to managers as now. Gen Ys and Gen Zs motivations are different to their grandparents by a wide margin. They are connected as a group and have formed into sub-groups like never before. Their collective psyche is tangible.

Over the last 14 years or so, I have watched my kids move through their school years. The positive experience they have gained at speaking with a microphone or performing in front of crowds, of exploring different media, of being told that each one of them is special and that every one of them can achieve great things is light years from my education where fear of embarrassment is one of my strongest memories. I have heard more than one of my generation say, "I worry about them when they get into the real world, they can't all be CEO."

I am astonished at the resilience of the youth and young adults I associate with. Embarrassments I may have feared in social situations are like water off a duck's back to them. Yes they have things that embarrass them; it seems parents will remain eternal sources of embarrassment, yet not anywhere near to the extent of my generation.

Are you managing Gen Ys or Gen Zs? Have you worked them out yet? Do you know what motivates them most? If you have and you don't have a term for it, it is called "intrinsic motivation". The inherent reward felt in achieving something. Have you ever done a 1,000-piece jigsaw puzzle? Why? Because it was a rainy day? Because you had a blackout? When you started it you may have had one or more of these reasons, however, long before you finished it the sun came out or the lights came on. But you still felt the need to finish what you had started, you enjoyed the challenge and you certainly admired the result. So guess what? It is not just Gen Ys and Gen Zs that are driven by intrinsic motivation, so too is the average person. If you are still not convinced, I recommend you read Dan Pink's book titled *Drive* where he unpacks what motivates us and repacks it into a number of very implementable techniques.[58]

---

58 Pink, Daniel H (2010). *Drive: The Surprising Truth About What Motivates Us.* Canongate Books, Edinburgh.

I know what you are thinking. Money is a pretty strong motivator. Yes it is, and in some organisations money will be more of a motivator than others. Think banking, in particular investment banking. And for some employees money will matter more than others. However, as decades of staff culture and engagement research has shown, money is not the prime motivator for the vast majority of people. Yes their financial needs must be met. You just have to pay people fairly, making sure bonus structures are based on measures that really matter to the organisation. From there you need to move on quickly to building intrinsic motivators.

The essence of intrinsic motivation is a challenge and what your talented teams need more than anything else is a challenge they can align with. The scale of the challenge should be dependent on both what you need to achieve and the capability of your teams. For some teams you will give them a mighty challenge like President Kennedy did with NASA and the American people when he announced the Apollo mission. For others you will choose a series of increasingly difficult challenges that your teams will handle as they increase their experience and confidence. In doing so you will be building your cascading success.

Focused people

It's useful here to think of elite athletes and how they succeed. Olympic gold medallist Alisa Camplin built a team around herself to help her succeed. She was extremely focused on the task at hand. Focused people is what we want to help create our destiny and to make sure our smarter strategic decisions end up smartest. However, another word of caution.

Focus brings attentive, caring and talented minds to bear on the challenges a team is confronting. However, sometimes trying to give people focus can go too far. The greatest example of this I have witnessed is with an IT department at an insurance company that I was helping by facilitating a series of workshops with the operating divisions. Time and time again the problems with IT came up. It was obvious something was broken. The divisions had a series of challenges such as, the lack of critical functionality that required time-consuming work-arounds, the inability to get information out of a system, or the risk of a compliance breach because the IT department was likely not to make a change to a system in time to meet a change in legislation.

Because of the pressure the IT department was under, the manager had decided his people needed to remain focused and to minimise distractions. So the IT department moved to a new, secure floor in the head-office building. No one had access to that floor except for IT and a few senior managers. Not stopping there, the manager decreed that the IT help desk would be run by email, no phone calls.

What did this do for the IT team? They must have had fewer distractions and therefore could focus more on the projects at hand, however, it did much more than that. It ensured the IT department lost connection with the business. They became a higher authority that could not be held to account. While team leaders raised problems with their management, the division managers simply toed the company line and said the IT department needed to focus to get the backlog of projects done.

The icing on the cake was that when a staff member emailed the IT help desk, the reply came back signed off, impersonally, as "IT support". The staff member had no idea who they were dealing with and what did that lead to? Arrogant and poor customer service. The IT support staff soon worked out they were anonymous to staff and they did not feel the need to be pleasant or understanding in their replies.

By the time of my workshops, there was obvious hostility towards the IT department and things were about to unravel. In fact, they did. Being an insurance company, the business was heavily reliant on IT. Within a year, profits had turned into losses and some large contracts were at risk. Fortunately, with the issues of IT highlighted, changes were made and the company turned around its fortunes within a couple of years.

Getting the right focus for your people is the obvious goal. It starts with a clear purpose and a clearly articulated strategy and is backed up by actions that reinforce purpose and strategy.

Unfortunately, when articulating a strategic decision to staff we are often too loose and meandering which leaves people thinking it's the same old strategy. Or, we go to the opposite extreme and communicate grand visions that leave people entirely unsure as to what the strategy actually is. If you are Australian you will probably remember Kevin Rudd's grand 2020 vision, which is an example of both extremes at the same time!

In 2008, within six months of his election as prime minister, Rudd held the Australia 2020 Summit where 1,000 of "Australia's greatest minds" would come together for two days to form a strategic vision for Australia across 10 core policy areas. More than 900 ideas were generated and compiled into a report for government to consider. A year later the government adopted nine of the ideas and none of the political, economic or social pundits considered any of the nine particularly innovative, let alone revolutionary. Worse still for Rudd's government, he began to form a reputation for jumping from one hot idea to another. Stories began to emerge where he had bureaucrats work long hours and over weekends to get reports to him that he promptly sat on and on occasion never responded to. The bureaucracy was in a state of confusion. You can well imagine the disappointment of the Australian people. Rudd's popularity soon began to wane, and then plummet.

Contrast Rudd's vision with Kennedy's vision of "landing a man on the moon and returning him safely to the Earth". The best communicators of a strategic decision will clearly articulate what the end game looks like and what is in it for all stakeholders. Kennedy's vision was reinforced through the actions he took to ensure long-term funding from congress and his personal interest and support of the program.

It could be said that Rudd's 2020 strategy was much broader than Kennedy's Apollo mission. Rudd's was most definitely broad when first conceived. He soon learnt that tackling policy initiatives on a broad front was too great an undertaking without absolute party majority at all levels of the legislature. On the other hand, Kennedy's seemingly narrow focus actually had a much broader agenda. It spoke to nation building, to combating the enemy in the Cold War and to the advancement of technology for the sake of technology and all it can bring to the world.

How do you apply a Kennedy-like common vision and focus to your organisation? First, I firmly believe a brief, clearly articulated, catchy purpose statement is incredibly valuable. It gives people that high-level goal they can aspire to.

Second, take actions that reinforce the strategy. Ensure there is a budget. Perhaps more importantly, ensure there is guidance. As we explored in the previous section, it is about having the right amount of policies, processes and systems, ensuring they are designed well and implementing them efficiently to influence individual decision making. Finding the right amount is of course the challenge. Implement too many or some of the wrong kind and you will de-motivate people. Implement too few and leave things to individual interpretation, and the variation in performance will be too broad.

Third, people learn from decision making. That is why we use case studies to teach, to help people to process information, to analyse and diagnose. And don't forget, the people in your teams that are creating your destiny are making hundreds of smaller decisions each day. Just one, or a group, can derail your strategy a little to a lot if you are not careful. Of course, it is okay for people to make mistakes; that is all part of the process of learning from decision making. It is about getting enough of the more important decisions right up front. So your mission is to let people make decisions in pursuit of purpose and when those decisions don't result in a good outcome, help them recalibrate and refocus so they improve their decision making and create smarter strategies.

Tracking change

As you start cascading your success, as your creative leaders start experimenting, as your talented teams start building bridges and as your focused people make more and more of their individual decisions to act or not to act, you need to be tracking change.

Earlier, when I was exploring with you the implementation deception I was highlighting the need for organisations to be able to measure and monitor their capability. I also said that there were other things to measure. However, don't measure too much; measure what matters.

Cascading success requires you to track change. To reiterate, by its nature, if you are cascading success you are literally emerging out of the success of one initiative and into another one. The more teams and more people you have cascading success around you, the more you will need measures to identify the quicksand versus the gold.

There are plenty of change monitoring methodologies, however their results are often inconclusive, not only due to the complexities of organisations, but also because change is subtle. While a project may have ended and several new initiatives may have spawned from it, often some other subtle change has happened. Attitudes may have changed, perceptions may have shifted regarding the utility or otherwise of an asset, a team, a process or a system. The result is that the influencing of individual and team decision making has also subtly changed. Collectively the change may be for the better, which you will want to grow, or it may be for the worse and require corrective actions.

You also need to track change at the implementation stage of your strategic decision. You can do so in a sophisticated way using software, or by simply using a whiteboard and taking a photo. The objective is to capture the important pieces of change and be able to compare them over time to pick up on the major subtleties. Mimic the technique of time-lapse photography, which captures subtle changes over long periods of time, showing you the changes, where and when they happened.

I mentioned earlier that the Australian Defence Department uses an approach where they identify the fundamental inputs to capability (FICs), where capability is the ability to perform operations as required by government. Their list includes personnel, organisation (organisational design), collective training, major systems, supplies, facilities and training areas, support and command and management. They monitor these FICs across the lifecycle of their major assets. Given that the lifecycle of many of these assets runs into decades – from concept to delivery, to operation to disposal – having a detailed understanding of their FICs and how they are changing through the project lifecycle is one way they have of identifying the subtle changes in delivery.

This concept will fit almost any implementation of a strategic decision, no matter how big. You can draw one high-level view of the landscape on your whiteboard and then draw more detailed views as you drill down for larger projects. Choose an appropriate length of time for the pace of change for your project and re-draw your landscape maps. What might you see?

Much of what you would see would be how effective your cascading success has been. Also, you would identify the impacts of changes imposed from external environments. However, one area I want you to focus in on is your equivalent to Defence's "command and management". This is where the key decisions are being made. Ask yourself, which decision makers have changed roles and how has this affected the outcomes for the project, now and in the future? Have decision rights changed horizontally as reporting lines have changed, or vertically as delegations have changed? Has decision making further devolved to the coal face or has it been concentrated in the higher echelons and why?

In Part V I will give you some tips on how to ensure decision making by your people, teams and leaders is optimised. You will learn to look for changes in what is motivating staff, whether they are doing the hard-smart work to clarify their options and whether or not they have fallen into the implementation-deception trap.

There are literally thousands of decisions following your one great strategic decision. Be on top of the quality of decision making all the way through. Watch it relentlessly and it will deliver the goals you have been planning to reach.

Part V

Decision time

Chapter 11

Smarter decisions

By now I am assuming that you have a pretty clear picture of the key flaws in decision making and you are interested in learning new ways for making smarter decisions and consequently developing smarter strategies. I have written about a number of traps to avoid and have given some suggestions for how to do the hard-smart work and what to consider when implementing key strategies. In this last part of the book I will provide you with a formula for decision making, and for identifying the type of strategy you should be designing for any given situation.

Do you remember the statistics I gave you at the beginning of the book? Paul C. Nutt, in his book *Why Decisions Fail*[59] unpacks decades of research into nearly 400 decisions by strategic

---

59 Nutt, Paul C (2002). *Why Decisions Fail: Avoiding the Blunders and Traps That Lead to Debacles*, Berrett-Koehler Publishers, San Francisco, CA.

leaders and found the success rate was about 50 percent. That is no better than chance. I also quoted some statistics from the systems-reliability engineering field that suggested for tasks that require a high level of comprehension and skill, the success rate is only 86 percent.

Think of the fall-out and rework that comes from getting 14 percent of your decisions around complex tasks wrong. Think of the wealth destroyed, the opportunities missed, by getting 50 percent of your strategic decisions wrong!

Decision making is a challenge. No question. There are no certainties in life. We cannot know all the possible consequences of our decisions. That doesn't mean, however, that we can't improve decision making.

What does improved decision making look like? Like life is a journey, so is the development of our decision-making skills. The old saying comes to mind, "You can't put an old head on young shoulders." While, through life, we are exposed to a myriad of skills to choose from and learn, our decision-making journey improves our ability to select the best skills to acquire and develop. Deciding comes first. It is the single most important thing we do and we do it thousands, or even tens of thousands of times a day. Each day in our business lives we make a number of significant decisions. And on a less regular basis we are called on to make strategic decisions. Decisions that will lead to thousands or hundreds of thousands or even millions of decisions by staff, contractors, suppliers, customers and competitors, all of which you would love to control.

Of course, that sounds impossible and it is. What is possible, however, is to improve our decision making down to the one-millionth decision. Under the broad heading of governance, we have been on a journey of improvement of our strategic decision making and strategy implementation. However, if you look at better practice in governance, you will find the principles and guidelines thin on strategic decision making. Some don't mention decision making as a key process, or role, for the board and senior management. Some mention it and call for "sound and well-informed" decision making. None I have found do more than acknowledge this need and mention the potential for bias that can come into a decision.

To deal with the potential for bias, the governance principles concentrate on executive and director remuneration and ensuring that there is a majority of non-executive directors on the board. They encourage remuneration arrangements for executives to be in line with the amount of risk taking the board desires. They also warn against options that will influence, or drive heavy risk taking to achieve the strike price for a big win, only to see the organisation crash shortly afterwards. They encourage arrangements for non-executive directors that are either a fixed-annual payment or fixed-plus shares, no options. This allows them to be more objective. And, with a majority of objective non-executive directors it should give the board the opportunity to make the best decision for the organisation, not for the directors or executives.

While this approach goes some way to addressing a major

threat to decision making – that is, the potential for bias in people's decision making – it by no means goes far enough. It does not adequately address the actual decision-making process. While the governance principles express the need for informed decision making, they do not provide guidance on what that actually means. To me, it means having a process that allows you to feel confident that you understand the risk in your decision making and that you have managed that risk to the best of your ability with the means available. If you have done that, you will have done more than pass the reasonable-person test used in corporations law. You will have improved your decision-making success rate. And not by just a few percentage points.

Think of what you could have achieved if you had made a better decision for even half of the decisions you have lived to regret.

DECISION TIME

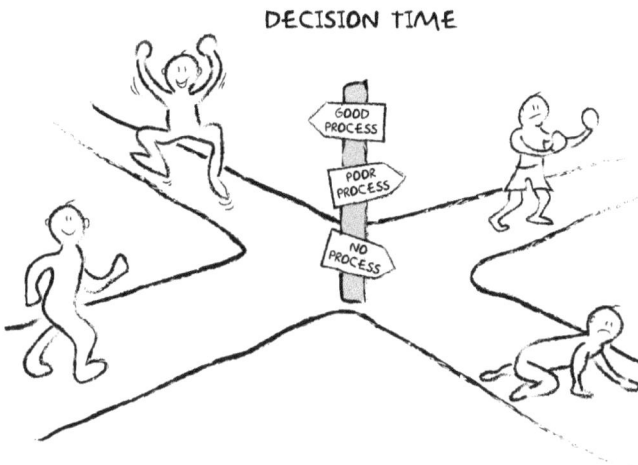

The MCI decision model

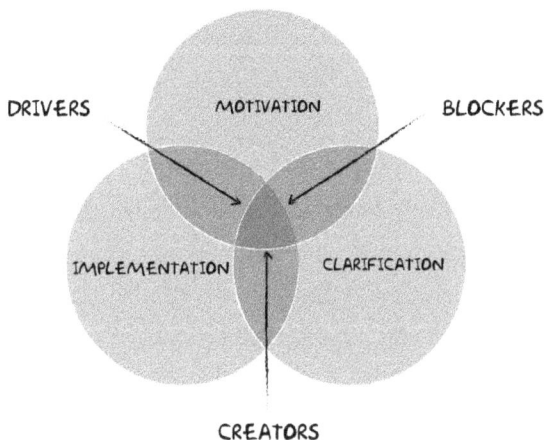

In order to manage the risk in your decision making, you need to understand the level of risk. The MCI (motivation – clarification – implementation) decision model shown below, and the tools I provide in these chapters to work with it are designed to help you discover not just the potential for risk in your decision making; they are designed to discover the extent of risk. The more the risk, the more you will need to take action to manage it. For some decisions you might not have to worry so much if the level of risk is high, as the consequences may be quite low. Take for example the decision to have an ice-cream. The motivation is of course self-gratification. If you are trying to lose some weight over the next month before summer comes, one little ice-cream is not a disaster, so the consequence is not significant. On the other hand, if you were a diabetic and you had not checked your sugar levels recently, it could be quite a different scenario.

MCI DECISION MODEL

DRIVERS   MOTIVATION   BLOCKERS

IMPLEMENTATION   CLARIFICATION

CREATORS

The premise of the MCI model is to flip our inherent decision-making process on its head. To start with motivation, then move to clarification and finally focus on implementation. This is inverse to our natural tendency to start with implementation, then do some clarification (after we have made the decision to proceed) and completely ignore the need to understand our motivation to ensure a good decision is being made.

Yes, our inherent decision-making stance is to immediately start thinking about how to implement the first idea that comes into our head. We start asking ourselves, "How am I going to pull this off?" Consider this: you are sitting at your desk pondering how to grow your business. The first idea that comes into your head is to start a blog and you start thinking through what you would write about and how that would attract customers. You may decide that doesn't sound like such a brilliant idea so you move onto the next idea which is a broader social-media campaign using Facebook and Twitter. Again you decide that is not such a great idea because your target market isn't very active on social media. Then you get the idea to use LinkedIn to get more of the right contacts and to start developing relationships with them. Soon you have developed a LinkedIn profile, you have started connecting and you are randomly firing off connection requests and in-mails. Wait up, what about stopping to clarify what a good LinkedIn strategy is? What have others in like-businesses done with LinkedIn to successfully grow their business? Don't stop there, what about all the other options you could consider to grow your business? Maybe there is a better way, maybe a coordinated approach across many platforms would be best.

And then there is motivation. Why are you thinking about growing the business? Is it growth for growth's sake? Is it for survival? Are you even asking the right question? Perhaps the underlying motivation is that you have become stale and bored and you have run out of steam. All that you might need is a break and a refresh to get the systems and processes that have been working for the last few years to work again.

Does this kind of scenario ring a bell? Do you get that sometimes we are not even addressing the underlying issues? So, the MCI model starts with motivation. It asks you to consider the key drivers motivating you when considering a decision. From there, with your motivation understood you can identify blockers to sound decision making, the ones that need to be harnessed or crushed when you are in clarification mode. When in clarification mode the MCI model asks you to dig deeply into what you are considering. It asks you to consider a range of outcomes, not just the outcome you first thought of when you started considering the decision. Finally, it asks you to think about alternative approaches. That is, to consider your options.

Finally, the MCI model helps you to unpack implementation. It asks you to think about how you will find and empower your creators, your leaders, teams and people who will deliver a successful outcome. It asks you to think about how, given all the issues you uncovered when discovering the motivators underlying your decision, and all the pros and cons you identified when clarifying the decision, how you are going to pull it all off.

So there it is, don't start with the question, "How am I going to pull this off?" Finish with the positive statement: "I am going to pull this off."

Before I go into the MCI model in-depth, and provide you with some tools to use to help uncover its power, I want you to know that you don't need this model for every decision you make. Of course you don't. Given we make so many thousands of decisions a day, how could we possibly stop and use a model each time? We would never get anything done. No, this model is a model for strategic leaders. Those tasked with setting strategy and leading organisations and teams towards fulfilment of that strategy. That isn't to say you might not use the model frequently, or that you would only reserve its use for strategic planning sessions.

On the contrary. You can use the MCI model for any decisions that you are grappling with and you can ramp its use up or down based on circumstances of importance and urgency. Once you get into the depths of the model, you will understand its power and you will be able to turn to it when needed, obtain a sound understanding of the risk in your decision making, manage that risk, make a decision and move on quickly and expertly to the next key decision you need to make.

One last note about using a model to help you with your decision making. Sometimes you don't even need a model to help with your tough decisions. Barney Smith, who lives in the Yukon Territory in Canada, once said to his sister-in-law who later became my wife, "If you have to toil over a decision, it is not a decision." He was helping her to decide whether to move cities for a boyfriend. She immediately discovered the move was not in her heart and she stayed in Toronto. Where we subsequently met and the rest is beautiful history. Long may it continue!

Unpack your motivation

In order to understand motivation you need to understand your drivers, the things that are propelling you to want to make a decision. In order to understand your drivers you need to think of them from three different perspectives. First is from the perspective of environment. In relation to the decision you are considering what is your environment like? Is it harsh, plentiful, obstructive, or supportive? Examples of harsh could be a poor economic climate or a CEO who is a bully. Plentiful could be that you are sitting in the research and development department of a company that has just made record profits and wants to reinvest in your unit.

Once you have considered your environment, you need to consider incentives. What are the incentives influencing this decision? Are you seeking some kind of physical pleasure? Are you looking for more intellectual stimulation? Do you want a financial reward or is there some other measure of success, like more self-determination in your life? For example, a potential performance bonus could be influencing your decision, or the possibility of a promotion, or a move into a more exciting area of the company. Perhaps your incentives are more altruistic, you can see how you may be able to make things better, create a happier team, get a clearer understanding of a problem, kick-start a step-change improvement in service for customers, or those in your care.

The final perspective is the one driven by your values. How much are your basic values driving your motivation around this decision? Is your motivation driven by your religious beliefs, an ethos that you live by or some other set of values that you were raised by?

Once you have explored all of these drivers, you can determine your underlying or dominant motivator from which you can identify the risks posed by various blockers. Below is a "decision dial" to help you identify where you are on the motivation spectrum from survival to desire to purpose. If your environment is particularly harsh, you are likely to be more in survival mode than not. If your incentives are very strong you are probably driven more by desire. Whereas, if you're thinking about this decision is heavily values-driven you are most likely motivated by a higher purpose.

Take the time now to use the motivation decision dial. Just like in the example shown in the dial, allocate ten points to each of the drivers – environment, incentives and values – in the score column, by multiplying the score by the weighting factor (10 for values, 5 for incentives, 0 for environment) and adding them up. You can now place an arrow on the decision dial that identifies where you are on the motivation spectrum. Zero is 100 percent survival-driven, while 50 is desire-driven and 100 is 100 percent purpose-driven. In the example, the total score is 60, which means that for this decision the decision maker is mostly driven by incentives.

Motivation Decision Dial

DESIRE
60

0
SURVIVAL

100
PURPOSE

DRIVER	0	10	Score	Weighting	Result
Values	Unimportant	Important	3	10	30
Incentive	Weak	Strong	6	5	30
Environment	Friendly	Hostile	1	0	0
				TOTAL	60

To use the motivation decision dial you may need some calibration. To score 100 percent survival-focused, your situation must be quite grave. Such as, if you make the wrong decision, or you don't make a decision, you will lose your job or your business. On the other hand, to say you are 100 percent purpose-focused, please take a minute to compare yourself to Mahatma Gandhi, Nelson Mandela, and Aung San Suu Kyi. Think of how they decided to endure great hardship when they could have led much simpler lives. All so that others can one day enjoy less poverty and oppression and experience the feelings that liberty brings. Now that is as near to 100 percent purpose driven as you can get.

Here I need to create a decision point for you. Now that you have your own personal motivation decision dial result, stop and ask yourself if you are answering the right question. For example, if the motivation decision dial points more towards survival than desire, you should ask, "Will what I am considering ensure my survival if successful?" or, should it be, "How can I get out of this organisation on my own terms?" If the motivation decision dial points more towards desire, perhaps the question you should be asking is, "If I pursue this particular option and I am successful, will I be happy?" or, "Is desire an appropriate motivator behind me wanting to consider taking this on?". And finally, if the motivation decision dial points more towards purpose than desire, the question you should be asking is, "Will my purpose really be enhanced by this initiative?" or, "Will I feel fulfilled in going down this path?". If you don't need to reframe your decision then read on. If you do, take a moment to reframe and then read on.

Motivation mindset. Given you now have an understanding of where you are on the motivation spectrum, what risk does your position hold? The first step to answering that question is to identify the "charge" created from your mindset. In physics, scientists talk about positively charged particles and negatively charged particles. Similarly, what I am talking about is positive blockers and negative blockers. Please look at the table below. For each motivational position I have identified two mindsets: one positive and one negative. It is now time to ask yourself, "Which mindset do I have for the decision I am considering?" If it is positive, the high-level risk posed by your motivation position is low; that is, you have a good mindset to clarify your options. Or, if you are in survival mode, you are willing to bear the pain to see the decision through. If you decide you have a negative charge, you have an elevated risk of either not seeing the forest for the trees or being frozen on the spot.

Don't worry if you have a negative charge, in the next two sections, I will give you the tools to manage that risk. It is important, however, that you are aware the risk exists so you can do something about it.

Table 5: Motivation mindset charge

MOTIVATION	MINDSETS	BLOCKERS	CHARGE
Purpose	Think what could be Think what must be	Must find options Sole focus	Positive Negative
Desire	Nice to have Must have	Open to options Narrow Focus	Positive Negative
Survival	Win at all costs Fear of failure	High pain threshold Low in confidence	Positive Negative

General blockers. While the motivation mindset charge is the headline risk for your decision, there is a host of general decision blockers that affect decision making. If your headline risk is high with a negative charge, it will be harder to overcome these blockers. If your headline risk is low, the main risk is that you fall into the trap of working too hard on identifying and managing blockers rather than getting on with doing the hard-smart work, then making the decision and then implementing it. With this in mind, let's explore general blockers.

For any decision we take we will naturally have ideas of our options and, through laziness or because we don't have enough information, we will make assumptions. We then develop theories about how each option may pan out. All of these, in particular the perceptions we form, are areas of potential risk.

The main sources of risk are the unconscious psychological biases each of us have, and which I explored in Part II. There, I explained that researchers in the fields of psychology and behavioural economics have identified scores of unconscious psychological biases, or risk factors. I explored the five most common ones. While it would be ideal to tackle every risk factor identified by researchers, the key to a good model is simplicity. So, I will only ask you to focus on the five most common biases which I see in almost every decision-making workshop I run. At the end of this section is a table summarising these five risk factors, my suggested solution, and the most likely best action you can take to manage the risk as you move into the clarification phase of your decision.

The five most common risk factors are anchoring, availability, representative, affect and confirmation (or AARAC). I have explained and defined each of these in Chapter 6, under the sub-heading Enough blocks to build a building. You may find it useful to re-read that section. But there's some more I want to tell you about these characters.

Anchoring. We have a tendency to anchor to the first number we hear in a negotiation, that is why a seller should always state a high but realistic starting price and a buyer should do the opposite, that is they should have a low but realistic starting price. See how the range has been set. Similarly, we will anchor to different pieces of information that we hear that are relevant to our decision. Whatever the key pieces of information are for your decision, take some time and look for a different reality in what may seem like a far-away place. I want to inspire you. We have a tendency to underestimate the possibilities, to think too short term. Only the special few could, 20 years ago, think of a future with smart phones and wearable devices. Go talk to sales if you are in engineering, go talk to the receptionist if you are from a regional office, go look in a totally unrelated industry that has a similar challenge, go read a book by a futurist. Think long term. Pull up anchor and sail to the other side.

Availability. When it comes to infrequent occurrences like shark attacks or hostile takeover bids, we hear and develop a skewed perspective of how frequent these events occur. Data helps up get things into the right perspective. It gives us the real answer. Take the Australian Shark Attack File (ASAF) curated by the Taronga Conservation Society Australia.[60] While there have been multiple shark attack deaths per year in Australia in the past few years, according to the ASAF, the long-term average remains about one per year and compares favourably with 292 deaths per year from drowning. Some eight fishermen per year die rock fishing and 23 people a year from diving. So, now, are you feeling safe from shark attack or are you generally feeling uncomfortable about Australian waters? Come on, there are more than 23 million people in Australia. The death rate from shark attack is, like, one in tens of millions and drowning is less than two in 100,000.

Dig a little deeper and we get more perspective. According to *Surfing Life*, the Australian Bureau of Statistics in its data release, for the years 2011-12, shows that 226,000 Australians participate in surf sports of some kind.[61] So the death rate from shark attack is closer to one in 200,000 given the vast majority of deaths are surfers. Still, because of the "availability" phenomenon, many people are more worried about shark attack than driving a car or being a passenger in a car where in Australia the death rate is about one in 20,000.[62]

60 From: https://taronga.org.au/animals-conservation/conservation-science/australian-shark-attack-file/latest-figures

61 Carroll, Nick (2014, May 19). "Lies, damned lies and statistics," *Surfing Life*. From: http://www.surfinglife.com.au/news/sl-news/11434-lies-damned-lies-and-statistics

62 Calculated from Dept of Infrastructure data. See: https://infrastructure.gov.au/roads/safety/index.aspx

My point is that data trumps intuition. You simply should not be fooled into thinking you know the likelihood of certain events if you have not done some digging. When the data is not readily available you may need to create it. That is why we survey staff and customers as two simple and highly prevalent examples. If done in a scientific way, the results are comparable year-on-year, and between business units and between organisations.

Representative. This psychological phenomenon, representative, is where we convince ourselves that what we are looking at is the same as something we have seen before and so our decision can be based on knowledge of the outcomes from the previous event. In Thailand they have a saying for tourists, in particular when selling "knock-offs" of popular brands like Rolex watches, "same, same but different". While something might look the same, without close inspection you cannot be confident it is. The best way to handle this potential risk in your decision making is to ask yourself, "What is unique about this situation?" and, "What makes it different to all the ones that went before?" And of course you must then ask, "What does this mean?"

Affect. If I like you, I am more likely to heed your advice. Also, I like sport, so if you use a sporting analogy to explain something to me I am more likely to accept what you're saying. The problem is you may know very little about the decision I need to make. Let's face it, no one is an expert in all fields.

For your more important decisions you should look away from those you admire and even those you love if they do not have expertise in the area you are considering. While mums, dads and old heads on old shoulders have wonderful life experiences, it does not mean they understand the potential upside and downside of all things new. Social media is one example.

One more interesting tip on the term affect as a source of potential risk. If you end up finding a range of people with expertise in the area you are concerned with, and you are getting conflicting advice, try what my friend calls the Three Stooges test. If you are old enough, or if you caught the biographical TV movie *The Three Stooges* in 2000, you will know the Three Stooges were a mid-20th century American vaudeville act where they kept stuffing up everything they touched. Moe, often the leader of the trio, would look to punish or query Curly's decision making by poking him in the eyes with two fingers. Curly would frequently end up with sore eyes. However, every now and then he would get his hand up and Moe's fingers would go either side of Curly's hand, preventing the poke in the eyes.

My friend was managing a very large IT project for a major newspaper. While they had plenty of good project management happening, often the technical issues were vexed. He said he was frequently surrounded by four or five advisers all with a different solution to the latest technical problem. In the absence of a clear pathway to confirm which advice was best and in the interests of time, he would apply the Three Stooges test and psychologically poke them in the eyes with two fingers to test the level of belief they had in their solution. The one who didn't blink, the one most confident after interrogation, would win his support. While this is by no means foolproof, he was able to make smaller, less critical technical decisions much faster.

Remember, I never said that decision making was easy, you need tools and methodologies to manage the risk in your decision making.

Confirmation. This final risk factor is a dangerous one. We like to be right, don't we? Well, the more we want to be right the more likely we will seek out information that will confirm our situation. We will even go so far as to disregard evidence to the contrary. In my role as a facilitator for executive team decision making, I say that part of my job is to unveil the elephant in the room, the thing that is obviously there, but no one sees it.

Table 6: Solutions for general blockers

Risk factor	Solution	Action
Anchor	Up anchor	Look for evidence in several other places
Availability	Data trumps intuition	Look for data or create data from talking to others
Representative	Same, same but different	Look for the unique aspects of the situation
Affect	Apply tough love	Look away, don't look back and find out what others are thinking
Confirmation	Unveil the elephant in the room	Look for the elephant in the room

The answer for group decision making is to get yourself a good facilitator to unveil the elephant in the room. For your individual decision making go see your most sceptical colleague, the one you think is always negative. There is no need to ask him/her for all their commentary. Just ask them if they think you are kidding yourself. People who always see the negative side will often concede the overall proposition is not a bad idea if it is not a bad idea.

Clarify your options

With the improved understanding of potential blockers to your decision making, it is time to do the hard-smart work. You shouldn't be afraid of the hard-smart work; you should be embracing it because uncertainty is the strategic leader's best friend. And, the only way to deal with uncertainty is to do the hard-smart investigative work.

In trying to tackle the blockers your motivation creates, I have already given you some ideas on where to apply your efforts. This includes searching for information in a different place, consulting with experts in a particular field rather than loved ones and consulting with traditional naysayers for a reality check. However, many of these activities will only supply information or opinion. It is up to you to turn that information and opinion into knowledge and, ultimately, into wisdom as evidenced by a wise choice.

Knowledge. The first step is the development of your knowledge senses. Just as we use all of our human senses to understand our world – hearing, seeing, etcetera – so too should we use all the knowledge senses available to us. We use our eyes to see, which is in a knowledge-sense observing things, our ears to hear which is to listen, our nose to smell which is a form of investigation, our sense of touch to feel which is to explore and finally we use our taste buds to guide our experiments with new recipes, which is a trial of new ideas. All of these are critical elements of our genetic makeup that have not only led to our survival, they have led to our evolution as humans into the intelligent beings we are today.

KNOWLEDGE CIRCLE MODEL

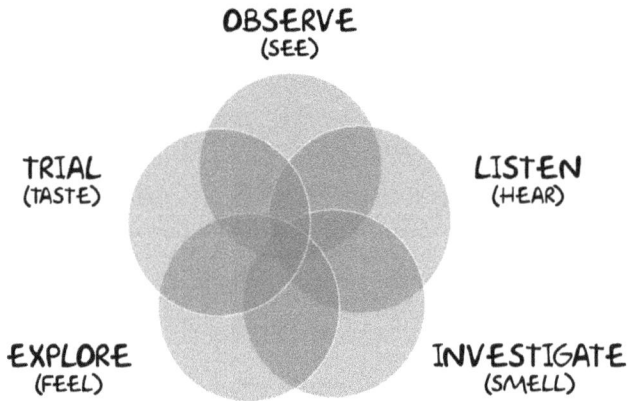

OBSERVE
(SEE)

TRIAL
(TASTE)

LISTEN
(HEAR)

EXPLORE
(FEEL)

INVESTIGATE
(SMELL)

Above is a diagram that identifies each of our human senses. All these senses form the core knowledge, or as I like to think of it, the knowledge sense. I set out below a guide to using all of these five senses to enhance your knowledge. Let me explain how to use each one in more detail.

Observe. Everything visible can be observed. While some things are invisible to others, to the astute onlooker there are secrets to be revealed. Secrets to success, to failure, to happiness. You must open your mind and the first step is to slow down and look. The best example is culture. The culture in a team, business unit or an organisation is observable. The way people dress, the factory or office fit-out, the way meetings are held, the marketing material and of course, the way people treat each other. Ask someone to describe the culture of the last place they worked and they will answer you quite readily with very descriptive words. They will find it harder to describe the culture of their present place of work, particularly if you are a work colleague, as cultures can be quite diverse with many sub-cultures. The reason they can describe the culture of the last place they worked is because the dominant elements have survived the test of time in their memory. Everything visible is observable, you just need to slow down long enough to look.

Listen. What is the hardest thing for a leader to do? Are you thinking: fire people, remain calm, manage conflict, make the tough decisions? I think it is something much more fundamental. It is communication. I truly believe communication is the single hardest challenge a leader faces. If you communicate well you will ensure the right people are hired and there will be no need to fire. Remaining calm will be much easier as you won't need to be exasperated at the actions of others and conflict will be the domain of the lunchtime sporting contest because staff will be standing side by side and nearly perfectly aligned with your organisational purpose. As for the tough decisions, they won't seem as tough as you will have such clarity over your options.

Listening is the first and most critical step in sound communication. You cannot make a great decision if you have misheard the problem or the choices available. And because every decision has a range of stakeholders' interests to consider, you need to consult widely and listen carefully.

Investigate. When I say investigate, I don't mean develop a research and development budget. I mean, don't take someone else's word for it, check it out for yourself. Go talk to the shop floor or to a customer or to a supplier. Or go find an old timer who has seen it all. Google it, read old reports. Run some computer analysis. What does the data say? Find new sources of data. Investigation has no boundaries. You need to decide how much investigation is worthwhile. Once it becomes the way you do things, you will know with more certainty where to look and how much effort is required.

Explore. Explore for new ideas. What have you not considered in your decision to date? And remember, a major failing of strategic decisions is that only one option was considered. Look for alternatives. While your activities: observing, listening and investigating, will have provided more insight, sometimes you need some help to open your mind. Look no further than Google here. Simply Google "creative thinking techniques" and you will find a raft of techniques to play with. Because I was introduced to creative thinking through Edward de Bono's books (as I mentioned earlier he is one of the founding fathers of creative and lateral thinking) I am always drawn towards his methods. Having used his "Focus and Six Thinking Hats" for more than two decades, I find I don't need to go to another technique very often.

While the first few times you use creative thinking techniques may seem a bit awkward, persevere; the rewards always come. If you have the luxury, use a facilitator independent to your decision who is familiar with using creative-thinking techniques. The results will more often than not astound you.

Trial. Please, please, please gather the courage to experiment. This could be as simple as walking into someone else's office and asking them if they would agree or disagree with your proposition. Okay, so it may turn out that they say you have rocks in your head and you see the error in your thinking and you may feel a little bit stupid. So what? Most people are more interested in seeing someone have a go at solving a problem than giving up or continuing to beat their head up against a wall. Having felt more than a little stupid at times when trialling ideas, I have learnt that the best idea is to go with several ideas and several options. While none may get the person's blessing, that person will acknowledge you are a thinker and for that you will be admired, and appreciated.

Better still, rather than trialling a proposition in someone's office over a chat, is to design an experiment. Remember the experiment I mentioned earlier, run by Greg Linden of Amazon where he introduced recommendations to people and huge windfalls followed?

Experimentation is incredibly valuable. Please think about how you can trial your different choices around a decision.

Table 7: Human Sense, Knowledge Senses and Action

Human sense	Knowledge sense	Action
See	Observe	Watch the people, process and activity and take in the little things like the physical surroundings
Hear	Listen	Listen while observing, listen to stakeholders, assess their views and their importance
Smell	Investigate	Talk to others, look back in time for reports, run some new reports, gather data
Feel	Explore	Use creative thinking techniques to develop ideas within options and to develop new options
Taste	Trial	Experiment with propositions and with logically designed experiments or pilot projects

Finally, go back and revisit your blockers from the previous section. Were your blockers positively charged, or negatively charged? Did you take the right action when developing your knowledge? Did you raise your anchor, seek out enough data, look for the unique aspects of the situation, consult with strangers, talk to the naysayers? If you have given it your best unbiased effort, then move on. If not, a little more hard-smart work is needed.

Wisdom. The final step is turning knowledge into wisdom. This can only be accomplished through analysis. Start with the data you have gathered via your knowledge senses. What is the data telling me? Next analyse the information from your stakeholders. What is it like if you were standing in their shoes? What does it mean for my decision? What have I learnt about our capability? How can I break that up into strengths to be exploited and weaknesses to be addressed? What are my options? How much insight have I gleaned so I can design a range of solutions that I can consider? How far can I go with a concept design without slowing the process down too much or using up too many resources? And finally, what appears to be the opportunity to innovate in developing the best solution?

Analysis has no bounds. It can mean working with numbers, with concepts, with stakeholders or with carefully designed experiments. My guidance on analysis, at least for this book, ends here except for this last piece. I have tried to be painstakingly clear throughout this book so that when I say things like analysis, like do the hard-smart work, I don't mean tie yourself up in knots, I mean do enough to be successful. Only you can know how much effort that requires. Sometimes you will get it wrong, however, the more you do the work, the more you'll know the amount of effort required. Sometimes it can, quite literally, be done on the back of an envelope.

Decision Frame. First, before you go into full analysis of an option, what it looks like and what the outcomes will be, you should stop and ask yourself if you need to reframe the decision. Are you asking the right questions? I asked you to do this after you properly determined your motivation, the driver behind a decision you need to make. Perhaps with all the knowledge you have gained your motivation may have changed, or you have realised that you may have been asking the wrong question. Take a moment, think about how you want to frame the question you will be answering and write it down. Now reframe your decision in two more ways and then choose the one that feels most comfortable for you. Happy? Let's proceed.

Outcomes. The most important aspect when considering an option is to have a clear picture of what it looks like. For each option that you are considering, write down what you think a good outcome will look like. My preference is to write it as: "A day in the life of …" where I consider the main players impacted by the decision and I describe their life after a successful implementation of my decision. Next write down the numbers, dollars if a financial decision, numbers of customers or staff affected are other examples. Remember data trumps intuition. Be numerate. Be definitive.

Level of wisdom. Now it is time to assess the level of wisdom you have reached. I use the clarification decision dial below. It covers data, stakeholders, capability, options and innovation which were the key words I used above to help you consider what type of analysis you might use once you have gathered data

Clarification Decision Dial

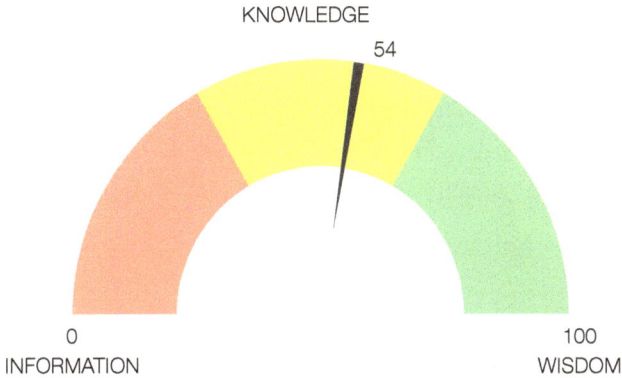

KNOWLEDGE

54

0   100

INFORMATION   WISDOM

Element	Focus	Scale	Rating	Score 1 is low, 20 is high
Data	Data trumps intuition	Absent to Sketchy to Interesting to Reliable to Definitive	Reliable – The data is from our existing systems. I am lacking the external data that would confirm my proposition	15
Stakeholders	Stand in their shoes	Opaque to Hazy to Clear	Hazy – Some of the key stakeholders were reluctant to talk to me	12
Capability	Cascading success	Amateur to Competent to Expert	Competent – The team has been developing nicely. Some work is needed to ensure all the team members gel	14
Options	Success by design	Suppressed to Forgotten to Searched to Explored to Designed	Searched – I did not make time to work through these and really understand what each option truly looks like	9
Innovation	Turn 90 degrees	Similar to Innovative to Disruptive	Similar – I did not make time to use creative thinking techniques	4
			TOTAL	54

using your knowledge senses. For me these capture the essence of great analysis.

For each of the elements in the decision dial, describe the position you feel you have reached and give it a score out of 20. In the example shown on the dial, the total score is 54, which is essentially a knowledge score and not too bad, depending on the importance of the decision and the potential upside and downside for each option. What you will need to consider is whether this score is good enough. If you are thinking about going out for lunch or eating in, you probably will be happy with your score. However, if this is a survival decision, you will be wanting to get as far up the wisdom scale as you possibly can get in the time you have available. If your score is not high enough, more analysis is required if you have the time. If not, consider options for delaying the decision or decide to only go part way with the decision and see how your decision pans out.

Deciding. In order to decide the option that is best for you, write down a worst-case and best-case scenario for each. Now think about how likely the worst, good and best outcomes are. Ask yourself, "If I made this decision 10 times, how many times would I get the good, best or worst outcome?" Perhaps nine out of 10, maybe only three out of 10 and hopefully a small two or less out of 10 for the worst outcome. Now overlay each of the options on an x-y diagram, like in the diagram below headed Find the Right Frequency. In the diagram, each option, indicated by different line styles, has similar best-case and worst-case outcomes, each with a different frequency of occurrence. You know this as each of the curves have a start and end point on a similar point on the outcome axis. This may not be the case for your options, which could heavily influence your decision. For example, one option may have a downside that is so disastrous you simply don't want to consider it.

In the example in Find the Right Frequency, the last option, skewed way to the right, is obviously the best option as it should, according to the analysis, most frequently result in very good outcomes and has fewer occurrences of all the lesser outcomes than the other options. This would be a no-brainer for the unbiased decision maker.

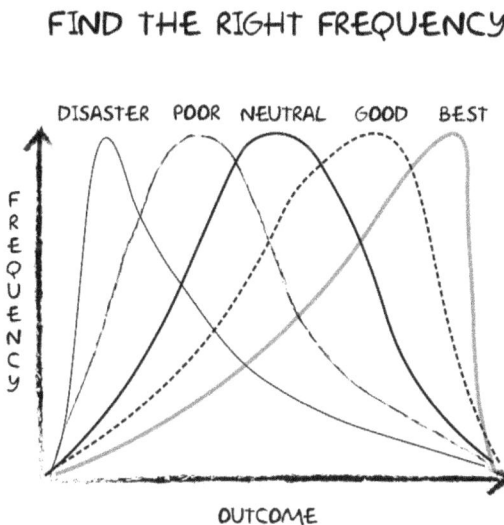

FIND THE RIGHT FREQUENCY

DISASTER   POOR   NEUTRAL   GOOD   BEST

FREQUENCY

OUTCOME

This exercise is intended to illustrate to you that we need to consider the range of possible outcomes for our decisions and their likelihood. If we do this we are unlikely to take a big risk unwittingly and we are unlikely to be able to look a gift horse in the mouth and reject it just because we like one of the other options better.

Now you have made your big decision, it's time to design your implementation so you give yourself the best shot at delivering, or even exceeding, the outcome you are seeking.

Design your implementation

For most strategic decisions the implementation will be quite complex and will occur over long periods of time. Hence you need to design cascading success. Don't think for a second you can set it and forget it. Remember, the value of one big decision is equal to the value of the thousands, tens of thousands, hundreds of thousands of decisions that follow only if those decisions are, by a significant majority, the best decisions for ensuring your big decision is successful. To give your strategic decision its best shot for success, take these eight critical steps.

Table 8: Steps to take for cascading success

1	Document your decision so you can't change the game for convenience
2	Articulate purpose so staff can align themselves to it
3	Craft creative leaders who are willing to experiment
4	Create challenged teams so they become self-motivated

5	Focus your people by ensuring actions are aligned with strategy
6	Measure what matters so you can track success and make adjustments
7	Close the loop by checking that what you will end up with is what you really want
8	Keep a record of all the bigger decisions you make so you can monitor success

Step one – document your decision. The first thing you need to do is document your decision. If you don't, you will give yourself the luxury of being able to reconstruct your memory at some time in the future, to shift the goal posts to suit yourself.

Step two – articulate your purpose. Second, you need to think about articulating your purpose. You need a catch phrase and an "elevator pitch". An elevator pitch refers to the amount of time you have to explain your purpose to someone when you're travelling in an elevator, about 30 seconds. The right catch phrase becomes almost like a war cry for the teams of people you will be leading. The need for an elevator pitch is two-fold. One, because it gives clarity to the decision you have made. Second, so you can explain it to anyone quickly and they will get the gist and, more importantly, the value. By anyone, I mean if you are the CEO then you can explain it quickly to an investment analyst, a supplier or a potential new hire. If you are strategic leader of a large team in a large organisation then you can explain it to the CEO in the elevator on the way up to your floor when they ask you what you have been working on. You can explain it to another business-unit head, if you need to engage them to get your project across the line. And you can explain it to a potential new hire so you grab that talent before anyone else does.

Take a moment to review the purpose statements in the section The power of purpose in Chapter 10 and have a crack at writing a purpose statement and reciting your 30-second elevator pitch. Here is one of my favourite examples that I use all the time to get my point across about the power of purpose, although unfortunately I don't know who to attribute it to.

I was told once that a five-star hotel chain had the purpose statement: "Sophisticated people serving sophisticated people". I can well imagine the hotel chain CEO's elevator pitch. It may have gone something like this:

> Our belief is that everyone who is treated with respect will respond in kind. We want our guests to have an experience, whether with the concierge or with our maintenance staff that makes them feel special, because they are special to us. If our guests feel special, our hotel environment will be one that not only our guests will love, so too will our staff as they will be treated with respect in return. We will be both hotelier and employer of choice.

Step three – craft creative leaders. Unless you are in the enviable position of being able to build your teams from scratch, you will need to identify your key leaders for this strategy and set them up to succeed. While you will be looking for leaders with the standard set of leadership qualities that suit your organisation, you need to identify those who show creativity as evidenced by their willingness to experiment. If such leaders do not immediately come to mind, identify the ones you feel you can develop into creative leaders.

To take a leader and craft them into a creative leader, you need to design some initial experiments for them, to coach them through the process, to help them measure the outcomes, to work with them to develop lessons from the experiment and to make decisions based on those lessons. Over time you will build their confidence as they will see how so much more can be achieved with a little experimentation.

Step four – create challenged teams. Talented teams are ones with the right mix of skills and attitudes for the challenge ahead. Given the hard-smart work you have done, you will know the skills that you need in your teams. To ensure the right attitude, in addition to relying on your team leaders to create the right team environment, you will need to ensure you set them appropriate challenges to tap into their intrinsic motivation. The challenges must be ones that each team can see is aligned with purpose and they must be significant challenges. They must also not have too much risk associated with them, either personal risk the team will sense from the challenges, or risk to the success of your strategic decision. This is where it may get a bit tricky and where you need to get the right balance between directed and self-directed work. Directed work is less risky and less motivating. The opposite goes for self-directed work.

Step five – focus your people. A focused person is one who understands and aligns to purpose and strategy and who believes in the actions they are undertaking, whether directed or self-directed. The focused person will help deliver the strategy and fulfil the purpose. The two key elements are to communicate your strategy and to ensure all of your personal actions and the actions of your team leaders are in step with purpose and strategy. Any conflicting messages will de-motivate your staff.

Now I just said that communicating your strategy is key to focusing your people. I mentioned earlier that communicating is the hardest thing a leader has to do. It's harder than firing people, staying calm under pressure, managing conflict or making the tough decisions, most of which arise because of poor communication in the first place. One of the best techniques for communicating strategy is to tell stories. You can bring your strategy alive by creating stories around customers, staff and other stakeholders that help everyone understand what it is like for them now, and what it will be like for them after you have delivered on your strategy.

Step six – measure what matters. You can't track progress and provide the feeling of reward for your teams if you do not measure things and set targets. The challenge is to identify what to measure and that means you need to measure what matters to the ultimate success of your strategic decision. There is no point measuring costs without measuring the benefits. What if you stayed within budget but unknowingly only delivered half the benefits you were expecting? While you need to monitor costs, you also need to monitor the progress towards the benefits sought.

When you are choosing what to measure in terms of progress towards benefits, ask yourself these questions:

- How will I really know if I am achieving what I set out to achieve?
- How can I know if what my teams are doing will actually deliver that result?
- How can I know if my teams are capable of achieving the desired result?

If you ask yourself these questions and consider them deeply enough you will know what needs to be measured. From there you will have to design a cost-effective way of measuring.

Step seven – close the loop. Finally, before you go any further, you need to check one thing. Now that you have a much clearer picture about who will be doing what and the outcome you are seeking, go back and check your original motivation behind your decision. Ask yourself, "Will that motivation and those key drivers really be satisfied if I deliver on this decision? Or might it be the case that I am creating a rod for my own back? Am I creating something I may live to regret?" Remember the old saying, "Be careful what you wish for!"

Given what you want, how might this change over time? How long term is the decision? Think long-term health effects, think changes in family responsibilities, think changes in financial situation – flexibility can be a beautiful thing.

Step eight – keep a record. Keep a record of how many decisions are correct and how many are not, to find out exactly how much opportunity there is for you to improve your decision making. Gamify it, by applying techniques used in games to motivate yourself. Set yourself a target of 95 percent success rate over the next two years and track your decisions over time. Identify which decisions you did the hard-smart work on and which ones you took short cuts in. By the end you will have worked out which types of decisions need more of your time and effort and which need less.

How ready are you?

We can't expect to be 100 percent ready for implementation straight after we design our implementation. Obviously we need to put some things into place so the actual implementation is successful. Below is an implementation decision dial. I use it to determine how ready strategic leaders are for implementation and to track progress over time.

For each of the elements in the decision dial, describe the position you feel you are at and give it a score out of 20. In the example shown on the dial, the total score is 61, which means you are well past the preparation stage and you are taking decisive action. You will start at different positions for different decisions. What you should decide early on is how fast you wish to ramp up the scale on the implementation decision dial.

Implementation Decision Dial

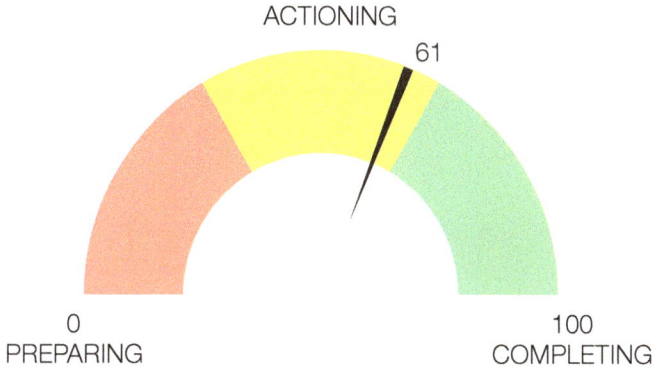

ACTIONING

61

0
PREPARING

100
COMPLETING

Element	Goal	Scale	Rating	Score 1 is low, 20 is high
Purpose	Clarity	Opaque to Hazy to Crystal	Crystal – Short powerful purpose statement that staff are using every day	18
Leaders	Creativity	Staid to Steady to Adventurous	Steady – A safe blend of creative and cautious leaders	10
Teams	Talent	Disunity to Skilled to Entwined	Disunity – Most skills are present, however the team are not yet sure of how they fit in and work together	7
People	Focus	Distracted to Aligned to Focused	Aligned – staff are aligned to our purpose but lack the team cohesion to allow them to be fully focused	9
Monitoring	Simplicity	Numbers to Statistics to Insight	Insight – we are able to measure what matters which informs our decisions	17
			TOTAL	61

This is a perfect place to end the conversation on individual decision making and move to the development of smarter strategies.

Chapter 12

Smarter strategies

What is the difference between a decision and a strategy? The strategy is the articulation of the decision. Take a typical strategic decision to move into a new market. One of my clients services electrical distribution networks, including poles and wires and sub-stations. They were looking at growth options, which included acquisition, vertical integration towards maintenance of power generation and horizontal integration into adjacent markets such as water, gas or telecommunications.

Their decision was to move horizontally into maintenance of gas-distribution networks as they had the processes, systems and safety culture for electrical distribution, and the market opportunity was reasonable. They were confident of acquiring the requisite skills for gas-systems maintenance so they ruled out an acquisition, or merger.

The first decision was to grow the business. The second was to horizontally integrate into gas and the third was to do so via skills acquisition rather than acquiring an existing player or merging with them. This third decision was their strategy. Their strategic plan was all about acquiring the skills, developing the relationships with the target market, understanding the regulatory environment for gas and overlaying their processes and systems from electricity distribution to gas.

The other decision they made was how aggressive they wanted to be in entering the gas market. That is, how much risk they wanted to take. They chose a low-risk approach and brought in a few key resources until they began to win small contracts, which led to the hiring of maintenance teams. They then went for bigger contracts and grew accordingly.

This example highlights a key challenge of strategic decision making and the development of strategies: determining how ambitious you should be with your strategy. In the example, a decision to have a more aggressive entrance into the gas market may have meant acquisition, or may have involved hiring more resources and going for larger contracts. What is needed to make a call on this is for you to determine the strategic potential of the opportunity.

Dial-up strategic potential

While I am sure you would like all of your strategies to be innovative trend setters that are disrupting industries, that is a big ask. Sometimes the resources you are relying on may be young, inexperienced and untried. Others may be old and tired. Or you may be operating in an industry on the wane.

The decision potential model below shows how I recommend you consider strategic potential. By considering capability, your appetite for that type of business and the scale of the opportunity, you are able to identify any gaps in capability, set sound objectives accordingly and design a strategy that suits.

DECISION POTENTIAL MODEL

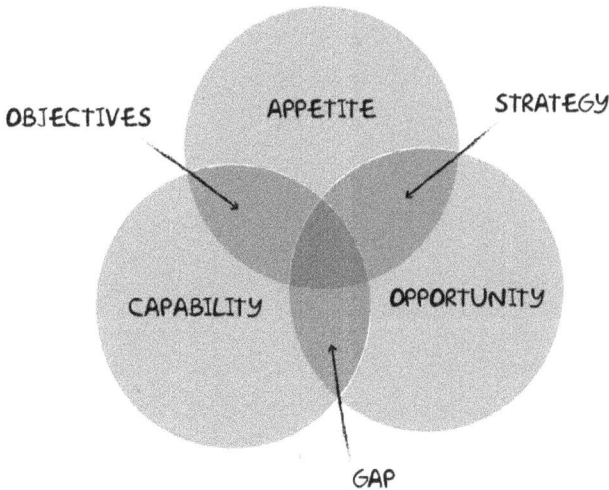

OBJECTIVES   APPETITE   STRATEGY

CAPABILITY   OPPORTUNITY

GAP

Capability. I have talked about capability a lot in this book. However, just to remind you, the concept of capability you should be considering is not just about culture and the skills of individuals and teams. It is the capability of your organisation or business unit as a whole to work towards objectives, and also to manage the uncertainty around them. Remember you don't just want good carpenters, you want carpenters that can handle a few bent nails, some warped wood and a design error or two.

Don't forget, when it comes to assessing capability, in the absence of a sound framework you will most likely overestimate and sometimes underestimate your capability. The other element of capability that is sometimes overlooked is how capable you are compared with your competitors. While on the surface you may have good people with good infrastructure, so too may your key competitors. They may well have the ability to mimic your strategy.

Appetite. The organisation's appetite for what the business unit does and where it does it, is a very important concept that many businesses fail to adequately think about and articulate. For example, if you are planning an international expansion, how willing are you to do all the hard yards of understanding and dealing with foreign regulations, foreign culture and possibly a very different way of doing business? As an example, many an organisation has found various parts of Asia to be a burial ground for their hard-earned cash. Or they have discovered that their staff made some poor choices in how they chose to conduct themselves and have played the game of fraud and corruption. The result, penalties for the company, resignation of executives and directors, and in some cases jail terms for staff. The larger your appetite, the more resources you should be putting into developing a cannot-fail strategy, providing the opportunity is there.

Opportunity. The scale of the opportunity you have right now needs to be clearly understood and not assumed. For example, the more inherently capable you feel your organisation or business unit is and the wider the gap between you and your nearest competitor, the greater the opportunity.

The state of the industry you are in is also a clear indicator of opportunity. Take the motor-vehicle industry. It is mature and highly competitive. However, the size of the opportunity is enormous if you can design a strategy that puts you one large step in front of the rest. The problem is that all of the industry players seem to know this and all are spending plenty on R&D. Consequently we have hybrid combustion/electricity driven vehicles, we have cars that can park themselves, we have the latest in GPS guidance and we have automatic breaking systems to avoid collisions. Still more money flows in and more outfits join the competition, including new players like Google and its driverless car.

On the other hand, newspapers are struggling. So much news is available online and for free. Cost cutting has been the norm with the inevitable decline in quality of content that follows. However, because of the sheer scale of the world of news, players in and around the industry are experimenting with new models to try and find the goose that will lay golden eggs for many years to come.

Gap. It might be stating the obvious, however, once you have established your view on capability, appetite and opportunity, state the size of the gap between your current capability and the capability required to take on the opportunity. If you look at your situation just as the head coach of a sporting team does, you will soon be able to articulate the challenge. Every team needs talent, however, they also need leadership and they need to be focused. What is the size of the gap for each?

Even if you have talent, leadership and focus, you are not guaranteed success. You need infrastructure. You need somewhere for the team to train. You need planning. A plan for getting fit, a game plan and a plan for learning the skills and teamwork required to execute the game plan. You also need to take care of their well-being. Outside of work all kinds of challenges are being confronted by your workforce. While you don't need to lead their lives for them, sometimes a little helping hand on their choices in life will mean they are ready, willing and able to focus on their team's goals.

Objectives. The objectives you set are very important because of the message they send. You need to set realistic, yet challenging objectives depending on the capability gap, the scale of the opportunity and your appetite for the business you are planning to conduct. If you set unrealistic targets your people will at best think you are out of touch and, more likely, will think of you as unfair and not worthy of their attention and efforts.

For some business units you will need to set nice, safe

objectives. You might be needing to develop their confidence or your trust in them. For others you can choose more testing objectives, and for a few you can choose very bold objectives.

Strategy. The last step is to determine the type of strategy you want to develop. Put simply, the bolder the objective, the more creative the strategy will need to be. If you have set easy to achieve, safe objectives the strategy will be vanilla, or plain and will only need to be well considered. In between requires you to guide the team on the level of exploration you are seeking, the balance between simply getting on with developing a coherent strategy versus the need to do things differently and to be more creative.

Developing smarter strategies

Once you have determined the type of strategy you want to develop it is time to bring in the MCI decision model – that is the motivation, clarification, implementation model. While you may feel quite comfortable in using the MCI model already, I do want to point out a few things to consider when using the tools associated with the model.

Motivation of others. The key to understanding motivation is to understand your drivers, and in the context of joint decision making, the drivers of others. The decision potential model asked you to assess your capability, appetite and opportunity. All of these are entwined with your drivers. A very low capability may push you closer towards a position of needing to fight for survival, whereas if you are capable and very purpose-driven you are likely to have a large appetite for any opportunity that will help you fulfil your destiny. And the scale of the opportunity acts as an incentive driver.

On the other hand, if you are a non-executive director and you are considering a decision with your board and CEO, the CEO may have very different drivers. For example, a CEO may favour acquisition if they think they will be named CEO of the new larger merged organisation as they may anticipate it would come with increased benefits.

Alternatively, if a merger meant their job was at risk, their motivation when considering a merger could be survival.

My tip is to run the motivation decision dial for each of the key players of the strategic decision you are considering and identify where they land along the spectrum from survival to purpose. Then identify their mindset and the blockers they may face to sound decision making. This will give you the best opportunity to manage the risk to the collective decision making of the board.

Clarification of opportunity. The clarification phase of strategy development should be checking in on both your capability and the market opportunity that exists. I have said enough on capability and the need for a framework to be able to regularly and consistently assess it. However, just as important is the need for clarity of the opportunity. While the knowledge circle and the clarification decision dial are the tools I recommend, when it comes to understanding the scale of opportunity for a strategic decision, you will find it helpful to ask yourself a few more questions once you have done most of the hard-smart work.

Here I set out five questions you should at this stage ask yourself.

- The first question is: What type of opportunity am I seeing? Is it core, complicated or complex? Core means a stock standard challenge with proven approaches to tackle it. Take mining for example. If the target ore or mineral is of sufficient quality and quantity and the location doesn't pose unusual problems then the challenge is core. Complicated means that it is not so normal or usual and you are going to have to work hard to solve the problems. For example, if the mineral has unusual impurities, or it is at a greater depth, or it is in a country with major political instability, then it is more likely a complicated problem. Complex problems provide the greatest opportunity because the first to solve the riddle will reap the greatest rewards. Think Albert Einstein, Henry Ford and Mark Zuckerberg. If the target mineral is on an asteroid passing by our planet, given your current capabilities, that is a complex problem! More realistically, would be, what is the untapped resource deep in our oceans and deep within the earth's crust?
- The second question is: What can I do to clarify the opportunity some more? What data can I analyse? What experts can I engage?
- The third question to ask is: Can I take out an option on this decision? Can I take a bite-sized chunk of the market

to test my hypothesis? Can I build a pilot plant to test the technology?

- The fourth is: Have I considered the time-horizon over which I should be making this decision? Am I thinking too short-term, for short-term gain when I should really be playing the long-term game?
- And fifth and finally: Is this an irreversible decision and am I willing to make an irreversible decision?

Implementation decision rights. The MCI model prompts you to design your implementation by identifying and establishing the creators of your destiny. The decision rights you grant your teams will go a long way to determining whether or not your strategy suits the capability gap you identified and the objectives you set.

If you want safe objectives with a considered strategy and your appetite is low for this type of business then you should not grant too many decision rights outside of the key decision makers. On the other hand, if you want creativity and agility and you want innovation and you are hoping for disruption, then you will need to grant decision rights to smaller and smaller teams.

It is of course a case of horses for courses. However, if you do want creativity and you do grant broad decision rights then you had better be sure you have clarity of purpose and of strategy. Failing to do so could lead to chaos with teams finding their creativity in conflicting directions.

Agile decision making

With or without broad decision rights you need agile decision making. If your decision rights are narrow you will need agility to keep the ship moving. If your decision rights are broad, you have chosen creativity over control and you are seeking agility.

What does agility look like? It is the ability to spot opportunities and to grasp them with one hand. It is the ability to identify threats and to act quickly and decisively. Agility builds organisational resilience.

In order to create agility you need to ensure decision makers are informed, that there is an agreed process to make a decision, and that the decision is adequately communicated. An informed decision maker is one who is clear on purpose and on strategy. They are clear on what the strategy depends on, and they have systems in place to measure and monitor key indicators.

To be clear, an agreed process for decision making is not the MCI model. The MCI model is a tool to help with a making a decision. The process for decision making that I refer to here is the organisation's process for decision making and it is made up of decision rights and individual delegations. For example, for some decisions you will deliver all the decision rights to one manager up to a certain level of financial delegation. This is because it is their core business and they are deemed competent to make appropriate decisions. For other decisions there may be a need to balance the interests of diverse stakeholder groups, and for this reason you may establish steering committees with representatives of each stakeholder group. Every steering committee will need a basic charter and its decision rights defined. The authority of the chair needs to be explicit. That is, they either have the final say or they don't, and the committee must defer to a higher authority if a consensus cannot be reached.

The last part, the communicating of strategy, is incredibly important and is deserving of a book in itself. Having said that, there are a few tips that you should employ at all times when communicating your strategy so that agility in decision making can follow. If key decision makers are totally clear on the strategy, they will be able to make fast, good decisions.

Below, I set out five tips on how to communicate strategy.

Paint a picture: Make sure you can envision what the end game looks like for management and staff. This could be through story telling such as, "A day in the life of ...", through an infographic or a simple Venn diagram, which uses overlapping circles.

Draw the journey: Let the people involved know they are on a journey and describe it for them. Tell them where they are right now, where you expect to be next quarter and then next year. Paint pictures of each milestone if the journey is complex or difficult.

Use Simple language: Although your strategy may not be simple, make it as uncomplicated as possible. Avoid any business or geek-speak and use plain language that your workforce will find easy to understand, clear and compelling.

Start close to home: Make sure your direct reports get the picture very, very clearly. It is difficult to communicate a strategy with total clarity to a large audience. It will need to be reinforced by your creators.

Visit the shop floor: Don't rely on every one of your creators getting the message right. Go talk to people and find out what they are doing and why they are doing it. Ask yourself, is that in keeping with the strategy you have articulated?

Chapter 13

Smarter organisations

I have taken you through the MCI model for making smarter decisions and a process to identify the type of strategy you should be looking to develop. The one thing that remains is to give you a view of a smarter organisation.

Being in control of your own destiny is a beautiful thing. If you are the CEO or a top leader of your organisation then you have the opportunity to be the person to make the calls and make a real difference. With that wonderful opportunity comes a burden. The burden of responsibility for leading others. As a strategic leader you are very much aware of this responsibility, and although you may relish the position of being master of your own destiny you do not neglect those that you lead. Even if you are not the top leader, you may be a manager with a broad realm of responsibility. Perhaps you are head of strategy, or governance or performance or risk, and your role is one of influencing leaders. Whether a strategic leader or an influencer of leaders, being a good decision maker or teaching other individuals to be better decision makers is only part of the job. The bigger picture is of an organisation that has developed smarter strategies at each key level, strategies which are being relentlessly pursued.

Again I take you back to Herbert A. Simon's view of an organisation.[63] Simon depicts an organisation as one established to fulfil a purpose and which is made up of people making decisions. Decisions to act, or to not act. Simon describes the role of leaders as being to establish the policies, processes and systems to influence decision making at all levels of the organisation so that the best decisions to fulfil organisational purpose are being made.

The following figure shows the scale of this challenge for organisations. Every organisation, despite policies, processes and systems has politics. The politics will more often than not dictate culture, which of course impacts on capability, the number-one ingredient required for a smarter strategy. And of course, within silos in organisations and within business units and within small teams there are politics. Hence there are sub-cultures and sub-cultures within sub-cultures. The larger the organisations, the greater the number of sub-cultures and the greater the challenge to effectively influence decisions.

---

63 Simon, Herbert A (1997). *Administrative Behaviour: a study of decision-making process in administrative organization*, 4th ed., New York; London, Free Press.

ORGANISATIONAL MODEL

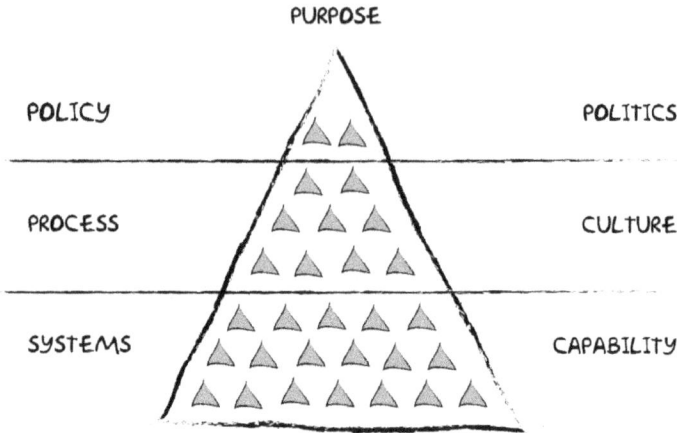

PURPOSE

POLICY   POLITICS

PROCESS   CULTURE

SYSTEMS   CAPABILITY

What is the best way for the strategic leader to ensure smarter strategies in organisations of any size, in particular the larger ones? By understanding the strategic potential of each business unit and by designing a strategy that is tailored to suit. My advice is to use the decision potential model at each level of your organisational chart where you expect key decisions to be made. Work with the leader of the business unit to determine the extent of the unit's capability, the appetite they believe the organisation should have for their business and the scale of the opportunity available. Together, with the right vanilla, explorative or creative strategy in mind you can formulate a plan that cannot fail, provided you have done the right amount of hard-smart work.

The other action you can take is to use a colour coding system on your organisational chart to help communicate a strategic picture to your leadership group and other key stakeholders. Use yellow for business units you wish to be operating with safe objectives and a well-considered strategy, green for those you want to be more daring and innovative and blue for those you want to be operating blue sky strategies. When you put this coloured chart in front of your audience it will paint a picture of the overall strategic stance of the organisation. Together you will get a feel as to whether you have enough of the safe, vanilla strategies in the right places in the organisation and if you have enough of the organisation seeking to explore and find more innovative, or even highly creative, strategies. The correlation is that you cannot expect major growth in a mature market without innovation or creativity and you can't expect to build a strong, reliable base to the business if everyone is into blue-sky thinking.

Quick tip sheet for smarter decisions and smarter strategies

The MCI decision model provides a simple process that you can use anytime, and anywhere to help you identify the risk posed to your strategic decision making.

However, you must remember – horses for courses. The bigger the decision, the more effort you need to apply to each element of the process.

Here is a quick tip sheet you can pick up for any decision you are grappling with at any time:

- Don't bite off more than you can chew, unless that is your only option.
- Don't rely on gut feel as your default position. Gut feel only works when you have lots of experience making a similar decision.

- Do manage the risk in your decision making by identifying the key blockers created by your mindset.
- Do think hard about your capacity to achieve your goals. If you have major doubt either take the time to find out more or take a smaller risk.
- Do turn 90 degrees. Always look for an alternative approach to the standard set of options.
- Do stay within your decision rights. They are there for a reason, good or bad. Get them changed later, but don't go outside them today without approval.
- Do take as big a risk as you wish to take and then execute relentlessly while keeping watch over the landscape as it changes.
- Do build in contingencies for the bigger risks you take. Create go/no-go gateways and options to invest more, or less, later. Keep technology and design options on the table until one becomes a clear winner.
- Do ask yourself this question before you proceed: If, after all the angst over this decision, after all the pain of implementation, will my world still be one that I will be happy to be in? Remember the old saying, "Be careful what you wish for!"
- Assess the success of your decisions. Keep a record and feed information back into Step 1.

While good, informed decision making will always remain one of life's greatest challenges, it is a worthy pursuit and I trust you will achieve more on this planet, impacting more people than you ever imagined if you take the leap and choose to improve your decision making and the decision making of other leaders in your organisation.

About the author

Bryan Whitefield runs his practice in strategic leadership from Sydney, Australia. His focus is on helping business leaders make smarter decisions and develop smarter strategies. While observing the seemingly exponential growth in complexity of information, technology and the possibilities available for communicating with staff, customers and other leaders, Bryan has identified developing decision-making skills as the number one priority for leaders to be successful in the 21st century.

While learning much from the many esteemed practitioners in the behavioural-economics, behavioural-psychology and risk-management fields and with his experience from his 30-year career as an engineer and advisor to executive teams, Bryan has developed new ways of tackling decision making and how to cement the success of those decisions in organisations. He has developed new concepts, new approaches and has relentlessly pursued the understanding of organisations and the people within them. His passion is for guiding leaders in how to make great strategic decisions, how to develop strategic plans that work and how to design organisational structures to meet the challenges of the 21st century.

Bryan's academic background in engineering and in business administration helps his pursuit of understanding. However, his practical experience as a shift supervisor and process engineer for chemical plants, and as a consultant to an array of industries across government, not-for-profit and the private sector, and as the Chair of the Board of the Risk Management Institution of Australasia, is what has positioned him to provide the kind of advice a leader seldom finds.

Bryan also writes a regular blog, publishes papers on emerging topics and hosts webinars and seminars to challenge his clients' thinking and to help them on their journey of discovery and learning. His website www.bryanwhitefield.com has a host of tools and templates designed to help you make the best decision you can.

www.ingramcontent.com/pod-product-compliance
Lightning Source LLC
Chambersburg PA
CBHW042310210326
41598CB00041B/7331